ISBN: 9781313200271

Published by:
HardPress Publishing
8345 NW 66TH ST #2561
MIAMI FL 33166-2626

Email: info@hardpress.net
Web: http://www.hardpress.net

Date Due

Library Bureau Cat. No. 1137

Cornell University Library
HB 161.M6315

Analysis of Mill's Principles of politic

3 1924 014 494 110

ANALYSIS

MILL'S PRINCIPLES OF POLITICAL ECONOMY

BY

L. OLDERSHAW, M.A.

Oxford
B. H. BLACKWELL, BROAD STREET

Two Shillings and Sixpence net

LONDON AGENTS:
SIMPKIN, MARSHALL, & CO. LTD.

NEW YORK:
LONGMANS, GREEN, & CO.
FOURTH AVENUE & THIRTIETH STREET

ANALYSIS
OF
MILL'S PRINCIPLES OF POLITICAL ECONOMY

BY

L. OLDERSHAW, M.A.

Oxford
B. H. BLACKWELL, BROAD STREET

MCMXV

NOTE.

Test Questions with references to sections in this Analysis will be found on pages 135—143.

MILL'S PRINCIPLES OF POLITICAL ECONOMY.

[N.B.—*All additional matter is placed in square brackets, e.g., this note.—Ed.*]

1. Political Economy.

Political Economy is a Science whose subject is Wealth, its nature, production and distribution, and the causes which enrich or impoverish mankind.

Wealth is not merely money, but all *useful or agreeable things which possess exchangeable value.* [In short, Wealth = all articles of value].

Another suggested definition is: Wealth = instruments. Everything useful is a means for the attainment of something else, *e.g.*, a field for the attainment of corn, corn for the attainment of flour, flour for the attainment of bread, bread for the satisfaction of hunger. Such a view is philosophically correct, but not sufficiently in accordance with the custom of language to provide a useful definition.

Errors respecting Wealth.

A. That it consists solely of money. This was the fundamental error of the *Mercantile System* which in consequence

    (i) Regarded importation as a loss to the nation of the whole price of the things imported.

    (ii) Looked on the Commerce of the world as a struggle among nations as to which could draw to itself the largest share of gold and silver in existence.

This absurdity, though none the less an absurdity, is rendered plausible because

(a) Wealth is always expressed in money, and it may be argued that what you spend your money on is not wealth but merely the use you make of your wealth.

(b) Money gives a command over the general fund of things useful and agreeable. It is the power of providing for any exigency or obtaining any object of desire, and is the only form of wealth which can be turned at once to any use. For this reason Governments especially are prone to attach almost exclusive importance to money, for they derive little advantage from taxes not collected in money.

B. That it consists of all useful things, *e.g.*, air. But air is free and therefore can command nothing useful or agreeable in exchange for it. Would air become wealth if monopolised? Yes. Would it then add to the general store of wealth? No, because the addition to the wealth of the monopoliser would be balanced by what was subtracted from the wealth of those who had to pay for it.

C. That what is wealth to an individual is necessarily wealth to a nation or to mankind. This is not always the case, *e.g.*

(i) A mortgage does not add to the nation's wealth. It merely transfers wealth from one person to another. When a mortgage is annulled the nation is neither poorer nor richer. All that has happened is that the mortgagee has lost so much and the mortgagor gained so much.

N.B.—A confusion such as is here indicated often leads to error in calculating the gross income of a nation from the Income Tax Returns. In these returns the same body of wealth is often assessed more than once. [The consequent fallacy is sometimes called the Fallacy of Multiple Assessments].

(ii) Slaves. If a man is part of the wealth of

a nation when he belongs to another man he must be no less so when he belongs to himself. But men are not wealth; they are that for the sake of which wealth exists. The individual slave-owner is only wealthy by the amount of property he abstracts from the slave, ∴, as in the case of the appropriation of air, no addition is made to the sum total of material or human wealth.

3. Differences in different Ages and Nations in:

(*a*) The Quantity and Kind of Wealth.

(*b*) Its Distribution among the Members of the Community.

(i) In hunting or fishing communities. (*a*) Wealth consists of skins, ornaments, rude utensils, weapons, canoes, etc., and land, but not to anything like the full extent of its value. (*b*) Wealth, or rather poverty, is fairly equally distributed.

(ii) In pastoral or nomad communities. (*a*) Add flocks and herds and the products of domestic manufactures and inventions rendered possible by (*b*) More unequal distribution of wealth, which gives the leisure that generates new wants and affords the opportunity for gratifying them to those more active and thrifty in acquiring large flocks and herds, or heads of families and others who get dependents to work for them.

(iii) In agricultural communities, which, historically, follow (ii), when the increase of men and cattle begins to exhaust earth's natural pastures. (*a*) At first these add to the previous store of wealth only the new products of the land as the population increases rapidly, and in maintaining it there is less leisure than in (ii), but arts and manufactures follow, but from different causes, according as (*b*) the governing classes take the produce from the first, as in Asia, or it is distributed among the small agricultural communities, which become the prey of larger ones. The latter process results at first in a race of conquerors owning the fruits of the earth and a race of conquered producing them, and eventually

(iv) In modern industrial communities, which vary very much among themselves; but all agree (*a*) in great diversity of produce, and (*b*) even greater diversity of distribution.

4. How Political Economy investigates these differences.

These differences must be due to causes. Where these causes are not physical but are dependent on institutions and social relations they are investigated by Political Economy under the heading of

(i) Production, which depends in the first place on physical laws which we take for granted.

(ii) Distribution, whose laws are partly of human institution, though their working is not altogether controllable by their makers.

5. Requisites of Production.

(i) Labour.

(ii) Appropriate natural objects.

(iii) Capital [which, being an accumulated stock of the previous products of (i) and (ii), is not mentioned by Mill in his first statement of the Requisites of Production].

(i) is either bodily or mental, or, in other words, muscular or nervous, and, as an agent of production, is always employed in putting objects in motion. The properties of matter do the rest.

(ii) is of very little use, except to primitive man, without (i). It includes, however, *powers* as well as *materials*, and the powers of nature, *e.g.*, wind and water power, are constantly and increasingly employed to relieve the work of man.

It is impossible to decide in any given work whether there is a greater proportion of (i) or (ii), and where both are necessary it is unmeaning to say that more is done by one than the other. This error appears in the view (held by the French Economistes) that nature is more important in agriculture than in manufactures. They were led to this error because Rent is paid for land; but Rent is paid, not for the greater services of nature, but, because land is limited and capable of being engrossed and appropriated.

This suggests a division of (ii) into

(*a*) Limited natural objects, *e.g.*, land in an old country, coal, water power.

(*b*) Practically unlimited natural objects, *e.g.*, land in a new country, water, air.

6. Labour as an Agent of Production.

Labour as an agent of production may be classified according as it is employed

(i) Directly about the thing produced, or

(ii) In operations preparatory to its production.

And it is important, in estimating the amount of labour which has gone to the making of the commodity, not to neglect (ii), which may take any or all of the following forms:

(*a*) The production of subsistence for subsequent labour [*i.e.*, Capital], but as it may be supposed that those who produce this subsistence have already provided themselves with subsistence, the claim to remuneration under this head is of another kind to that claimed by the five remaining classes of indirect labourers, *i.e.*, it is remuneration for abstinence, not for labour.

(*b*) The production of materials, *e.g.*, the *extractive* industry of the mines, the labour of growing materials like flax, cotton, etc., and the finished products of many industries which are the materials of others, *e.g.*, the making of thread.

(c) The production of tools and implements, which, unlike the produce of (b), can be used repeatedly.

(d) The protection of the producer, *e.g.*, the building of warehouses, the labour of the herdsman, the soldier, the policeman, the judge. Some of these classes are not employed exclusively in the protection of industry and are not paid directly by the producer, but they save the producer labour and are paid indirectly through taxation.

(e) The transport and distribution of the produce, *e.g.*, carriage of various kinds, construction of the implements of transport, of roads, etc., commerce, wholesale and retail.

Two other forms of labour, more indirect still, and subject in most cases to different kinds of remuneration, may be added.

(f) Labour relating to human beings, *e.g.*, the case of the mother, education, doctoring.

(g) Invention and discovery.

N.B.—The popular division of labour into agricultural, manufacturing and commercial, is of no scientific value because of the difficulty of drawing hard and fast lines between the different classes. Thus the "agricultural interest" includes the farmer, the miller, the baker, etc., but is the miller, *e.g.*, an agriculturist or a manufacturer?

7. Unproductive Labour.

Labour does not produce objects but utilities, which are

(i) Fixed and embodied in material objects.

(ii) Fixed and embodied in human beings, *e.g.*, doctor's work.

(iii) Mere services rendered, *e.g.*, musicians.

Productive labour is that which produces (i), not (ii), save indirectly, not (iii) at all. But it must not be thought that any disparagement is implied in using the term unproductive. Nor has the consumption of an object when produced anything to do with productivity of the labour exerted. Consumption too may be productive and unproductive. Whoever contributes nothing, directly or indirectly, to production is an unproductive consumer.

[*N.B.*—This distinction as regards labour is little used now.]

8. What is Capital?

Only the rude beginnings of industry can be carried on without a stock, previously accumulated, of the products of former labour. Thus this stock, which is called Capital, soon becomes one of the requisites of Production (*supra* § 3).

A. Capital = *wealth appropriated to reproductive employment*. It is what labourers live on and work with while they are producing more wealth. It is not therefore money, which cannot in itself afford any assistance to production. Nor is it any particular kind of commodity, for the distinction between Capital and Not Capital does not lie in the kind of commodities but in the mind of the Capitalist—in his will to employ them for one purpose rather than for another. Thus all the produce of a country devoted to production is Capital.

B. The whole of the Capital of a country is devoted to production, but it is not always *employed* in production. It may sometimes be diverted from the purpose for which it is intended. This occurs in the following cases:

(*a*) Capital consisting of unsold stock.

(*b*) Capital depleted by taxation.

(*c*) Capital depleted by the payment of rent in advance.

(*d*) That part of the Capital advanced to labour which does not support it but merely remunerates it.

(*N.B.*— It is assumed that Labourers *are subsisted from* Capital even when it is not advanced by the Capitalist, but when, *e.g.*, the Peasant Proprietor subsists on last year's produce till this year's harvest).

C. It is necessary to distinguish what is virtually Capital to the individual from what is actually Capital to the nation. Thus the £1,000 which A lends to B, a farmer or manufacturer, who uses it productively, is actual Capital, but if A lends it to B, a spendthrift, who consumes it unproductively, it ceases to be Capital, even if A has a mortgage on B's land and is in consequence no worse off than before. In the former case so much real Capital has just changed hands for the purpose of employment; in the latter case it has been destroyed.

9. Fundamental Propositions regarding Capital.

A. *Industry is limited by Capital.* This is implied in such metaphorical phrases as " applying Capital " to an employment and " the productive powers of Capital," but it is often forgotten that there can be no more industry than is supplied with materials to work up and food to eat, *i.e.*, than is supplied with a portion of the produce of past labour. Hence it is sometimes believed that a government can create industry directly.

(i) By making the people more industrious.

(ii) By prohibiting foreign importation, a measure which only transfers Capital from one employment to another; except in the case of domestic [*i.e.*, home] manufactures which can be carried on without much additional Capital because the people who engage in them are being fed already.

But industry does not always reach the limit set by Capital (*e.g.*, sometimes in new Colonies), sometimes owing to scarcity of labour and sometimes owing to unproductive consumption [*i.e.*, people "living on their Capital"]. In these cases a government may create industry, either

(*a*) By importing labour; or

(*b*) By taxes on incomes and the use of the proceeds in productive employments, or, what is nearly equivalent,

(*c*) By paying off the public debts, which gives the fundholder a sum he will use productively.

Now Capital, and so industry, can be indefinitely increased, and the produce will not, as Malthus has urged, be so much waste, because, even if population is not increased to share the increased pruduce of necessaries, there may ensue a wider distribution of luxuries. The limit of wealth is never deficiency of consumers.

B. *Capital is the result of saving.*

Even those who live on what they produce till they produce more must save what is necessary for this purpose, and certainly what anyone employs in supporting other labour than his own must be saved, but the person who controls what is saved is not necessarily the producer; he may be the latter's plunderer or task master.

C. *Capital is consumed.*

Either slowly in tools or buildings or rapidly in subsistence, while fresh Capital is being produced. Therefore the Capitalist is not to be regarded as a person who hoards in contrast to the beneficent spendthrift who spends money. The former spends productively, the latter unproductively (except that part of his wealth which gets in large quantities into the hands of people, stewards and the like, who use it as Capital). Capital must be consumed to reproduce itself, and this perpetual consumption and reproduction (and not the strength of the principle of saving) is the explanation of the *vis medicatrix natura* which enables a country devastated by war to recover its prosperity in a short time. For the greater part of Capital must be by the nature of things reproduced annually.

Compare the different economic results of the Napoleonic wars in England and France.

(i) England diverted hundreds of millions of Capital from productive employment but employed comparatively few additional men. The Capital was not taken from tools and buildings, it must have been taken from what paid labour. Therefore labourers suffered, but as the Capital could be reproduced quickly the Capitalists prospered and the permanent productive resources did not fall off.

(ii) France got resources from without, never from within. Hence high wages, injury to employers, and a general loss in wealth, owing to the great diminution of productive labour.

From this it would appear to be an argument against meeting a large unproductive expenditure by a loan raised within the year; that it is the labourers who bear the year's burden. This is true where the value so absorbed would otherwise have been employed in productive industry within the country, but this is not necessarily the case (*infra*, § 47 and § 54 A).

D. *Demand for commodities is not demand for labour.*

In other words, that which supports or employs unproductive labour is the Capital expended in setting it to work and not the demand of purchasers for the produce of the labour when completed. That demand only determines the *direction* of the labour. There is, for example, no particular preference on the part of Capital for making velvet, and, if there is no demand for velvet, the Capital employed in making it will make something else. (This is leaving out of consideration the effect of a sudden change). If a man uses his income in buying services he is directly benefiting the labouring classes, but if he uses it in buying commodities he is simply directing a certain amount of someone else's Capital into producing that particular commodity—which would otherwise be free for other employment, *i.e.*, in the first case he is creating a second fund of Capital; in the second case he is merely making use of one existing fund. But does he not in the second case, *i.e.*, in purchasing commodities, set free a fund of Capital which would otherwise be locked up in, *e.g.*, a stock of velvet? Yes, but the argument implied in this confounds the effects arising from the suddenness of a change with the effects of the change itself. Increased employment would not be given to labour if the use of the income for purchasing services did not free the Capital that would be used in making the velvet. But if the Capital was so freed, if, *e.g.*, the velvet maker had notice that there would be less demand for velvet, his Capital might be employed elsewhere, and there would be two funds of Capital where there was one before, for it may be said that the velvet-makers and the velvet-buyers have only one Capital between them. Thus a person does good to labourers, not by what he consumes on himself but solely by what he does not so consume.

There are two exceptions to be noted:

(i) A demand for commodities which can be produced by labour supported but not fully occupied may stimulate this labour to increased exertions. But this result is brought about without the use of fresh Capital or by a small new Capital for tools and materials expressly provided out of savings and not withdrawn from other occupations.

(ii) An increased demand for a particular commodity leading to an extension of the market in that commodity may produce a development of the division of labour resulting in an increase of productive efficiency (*infra*, § 13). In other words, in such a case the same Capital may produce more and so indirectly cause an increase of Capital with an eventual increase of the remuneration of labour.

N.B.—These fundamental principles expose a common fallacy respecting taxation which takes many forms, *e.g.*, that income-tax falls on the poor because it diminishes the spending capacity of the rich. It would injure the poor if it diminished the amount that would otherwise be set aside for Capital, but it does not, according to our principles, if it only diminishes the amount that the rich man spends on himself. No one is benefited by more consumption except the person who consumes. To know who is the sufferer by a tax we must understand whose consumption will have to be retrenched.

[Propositions A. and C. have been attacked as depending for their validity on the Wage Fund Theory (*infra*, § 25 A Note).]

10. Circulating and Fixed Capital.

A. *Circulating Capital* is Capital which fulfils the whole of its office by a single use, *e.g.*, materials, wages. It is so-called because it has to be constantly renewed and does its work not by being kept but by changing hands.

B. *Fixed Capital* consists of instruments of production of a more or less permanent character. Some kinds of Fixed Capital need periodical renewal, *e.g.*, implements and buildings. Some kinds need only occasional outlay to keep them up, *e.g.*, docks and canals. The most permanent kinds are those employed in giving increased productiveness to the land, *e.g.*, the draining of the Bedford

Level. In the latter cases, though Capital is consumed in maintaining the labourers employed in the work and in the wear and tear of their tools, a permanent result has been left in the land by co-operation with it, and the Capital cannot be withdrawn, so that the remuneration for its use comes to depend upon the laws which govern the recompense to natural agents, *i.e.*, rent (*infra*, § 27).

Now it is clear that A needs to be reproduced with profit as the result of a single use, while this is not necessary in the case of B. Hence it follows that all increase of B when taking place at the expense of A must be, at least temporarily, injurious to the working classes, for it is A, or the greater part of A, that alone supports the labourer, *e.g.*, if a man devotes to effecting improvements on his land half the Capital he has previously used in supporting labour, either he will only be able to support half the number of men he has supported before, or, if he borrows the deficit, he will only be using an amount of Capital already destined to support labour, not creating a new amount.

A particular aspect of this problem may be put into the form of a question:

11. Does the Introduction of Machinery injure the Working Classes?

It is generally admitted that the introduction of machinery injures the working classes in the particular department of industry to which the change applies. But that it does not injure the working classes as a whole is urged by some people on the following grounds:

> (i) That the cheapening of the product by means of the introduction of machinery causes such an increase in the demand for it as ere long to call for the employment of an even greater number of people than before, *e.g.*, after the invention of printing, printers and compositors were soon employed in greater numbers than the copyists they had replaced.

(ii) That the cheapening of a particular product enables consumers to augment their consumption of others, thus creating a demand for other kinds of labour.

To (i) it may be replied that the Capital used in supplying the new machinery (*e.g.*, the printing presses) is not available for supporting labour, and if Capital is withdrawn from other employments to support the increased labour, how much better off is labour as a whole?

(ii) depends on the fallacy that demand for commodities is the same thing as demand for labour (*supra*, § 9 D).

As things are, however, improvements are seldom injurious, even temporarily, to the working classes in the aggregate, ∴

(*a*) They are generally gradual.

(*b*) They are seldom made by withdrawing Circulating Capital but by using the annual increase.

(*c*) Great increases of Fixed Capital only take place in countries where Circulating Capital is also rapidly increasing, because the three elements that go with a readiness to sacrifice an immediate for a distant object, such as is involved in laying down machinery, are the three elements of a society rapidly progressive in the "effective desire of accumulation" (*infra*, § 16 A).

(*d*) Every improvement, even if for the time it diminish the Circulating Capital and the gross produce, ultimately makes room for a larger amount of both, partly because an improvement usually promotes the accumulation of Capital, and partly because it extends the limit that may be set to the accumulation of Capital (*infra*, § 47, 2) and to the increase of production from the land.

Yet there is nearly always injury to a particular set

of workmen, and may be injury to workmen in general, by the introduction of machinery, and the State should be on its guard against it.

There would be the same injury to the working classes if that part of Circulating Capital which is devoted to materials were augmented at the expense of that part which is devoted to the subsistence of labour, but this is not likely to happen, rather the reverse.

N.B.—A stock of finished goods in a warehouse may be Capital as to its destination, but is not yet Capital in actual exercise.

12. Degree of Productiveness of Productive Agents.

The productive efficacy of these agents of production varies greatly at various times and places. What are the causes of superior productiveness? They are

(i) *Natural advantages*, such as fertility of the soil, favourable climate (which affects the efficacy of labour as well as of the natural agents), mineral productions, a maritime situation and great navigable rivers (the last two often more than counterbalancing deficiencies in the first three).

(ii) *Greater energy of labour*, which often exists in inverse ratio to favourable climate, whose effect may be to enervate labour unless counterbalanced, *e.g.*, by the rigid military discipline of the Greeks and the Romans.

(iii) *Superior skill and knowledge*, either tending to inventing (machinery, steamships, etc.) or to increasing the usefulness of the individual labourer. Hence the importance of education (in making labourers more valuable) and particularly of a careful general education, which extends capacities beyond any special employment. (Cf. the evidence of Mr. Escher of Zurich on the varying capacities of the labourers of different European nations).

(iv) *Moral qualities*, e.g., *trustworthiness, etc.*, not

only in the labourer but in the community generally, as saving the expenditure on the unproductive labour of supervision (over-seers, police, etc.). Consider the waste occasioned to society by its members being unable to trust one another, in such matters as providing goods up to sample, especially in export trade and, per contra, the advantages of confidence which may be illustrated by the continuance of foreign trade between England and the Continent during the Napoleonic War, when, owing to the Berlin decrees, continental houses could not openly trade with England, but gave orders (which were executed) without any formal pledge of payment.

(v) *Security, i.e.*, both protection *by* the Government and, more important still, protection *against* the Government, especially in the matter of excessive taxation.

(vi) *Combination of labour*, which is one of the principal causes of superior productiveness.

13. Co-operation or Combination of labour,

Which, as Wakefield first pointed out, is a more comprehensive thing than that part of it widely known as "Division of Labour," and is of two kinds, viz.:

A. *Simple co-operation*, which is the combination of several labourers to help each other in the same set of operations, *e.g.*, two men pulling at a rope, a form of co-operation which anyone can understand and appreciate.

B. *Complex co-operation*, which is the combination of several labourers to help one another by a division of operations, either

(i) In the *separation of employments*, which is the first step in industrial development, when, for example, a body of men having combined their labour to raise more food than they require, *another* body of men are induced to combine their labour for the purpose of producing more clothes than they require. The influence of such separation on production is important. If the first body of men had to make their own clothes as well as till the soil, etc., their production would be slow and scanty. A body of artificers coming among a body of agriculturalists stimulates the productive power of the latter in a variety of ways, and at the same time constitutes a *market* for surplus agricultural produce. This market for commodities does not, of course, constitute employment for labour: it simply calls labour into increased vigour and efficiency. Hence the importance of a town (*i.e.*, a non-agricultural) population in an agricultural community, a point, according to Wakefield, that should be considered in any theory of colonization. The backwardness of India, productively, is due (says Mill in 1848) to a deficiency of town population, which is in its turn due to few wants of cultivators, and the best way out of this vicious circle is by a rapid growth of export of agricultural produce. [Manufactures have grown up since Mill's time, notably in Bombay.] Or

(ii) In *Division of Labour*. Cf. Adam Smith's description of the 18 operations of pin-making and Say's description of 30 workmen producing 15,500 playing cards a day by confining each workman to one or two distinct operations, while if each did all the requisite operations himself the 30 men would only produce about 60 cards. The advantages gained by Division of Labour are thus enumerated by Adam Smith:

(*a*) The *greater dexterity* of the individual workman. This is obvious. Great skill comes from practice, and the advantage includes not only greater efficiency but also diminished loss of time and waste of material in learning the art.

(*b*) The *saving of time* lost in passing from

one employment to another. This is an advantage that may be exaggerated. Few workmen change their work and their tools oftener than a gardener. Is he usually incapable of vigorous application? Moreover, though mechanical facility may be acquired by the constant performance of the same operation, does not a change of muscular or mental labour provide rest, and is not the habit of versatility able to be acquired like other habits?

(c) Increase of *inventions*, owing to the concentration of a workman on some particular branch of employment. But even here exclusiveness carried too far may be unfavourable to the cultivation of intelligence, and so more may be lost than gained in this respect.

(d) An advantage not mentioned by Adam Smith is the possibity under Division of Labour of a more economical distribution of labour by *classing* workpeople according to their capacity.

Division of Labour is limited

(a) By the extent of the market. It is no good separating the employment in pin-making so as to make 48,000 a day if only 24,000 are demanded. Markets are limited for various reasons: small or scattered population, difficulty of carriage, poverty, etc. They extend with the growth of civilization.

(b) By the nature of the employment, *e.g.*, agriculture. A man who only practised one agricultural operation might be idle eleven months of the year.

14. Production on a large *v.* Production on a small scale.

A. In the case of *Manufactures* the advantages are almost wholly on the side of production on a large scale. ∴

(i) If the scale of enterprise is large enough to bring many labourers together and the capital large enough to maintain them, it is possible to gain the full benefits of Combination of Labour.

(ii) Expenses do not increase proportionably to the quantity of the business.

(iii) Expensive machinery may be obtained.

(*Per contra*, it may be said that there is a greater attention to details in a small than in a large business).

Production on a large scale is rendered possible by *the joint-stock principle*, which has the following advantages :—

(*a*) Large capital.

(*b*) It may be employed in undertakings which individuals cannot perform with certainty and on a large enough scale, *e.g.*, banking, insurance, mail-steamers.

(*c*) Publicity, which can always be and ought always to be compulsory in joint-stock undertakings.

Its disadvantages are—

(*a*) Its managers are usually hired servants, and the work suffers through not being carried on under a "master's eye."

(*b*) There may be a disregard of small gains and small savings.

(Adam Smith is against it altogether, except banking, &c., but it should be remembered that managers need not be wholly paid by fixed salaries, but can be given a share in the profits and so have the interest of masters in the business).

B. In the case of *Agriculture* the advantages of large farming or *grande culture* over small farming or *petite culture* are not so clear.

The disadvantages of the small farmer are said to be—

(*a*) Poor buildings, owing to lack of capital.

(*b*) Scanty stock for the same reason, but it may be pointed out, from the example of Flanders, that a small farm and a badly stocked farm are not necessarily synonymous.

(*c*) Inferiority of skill and knowledge.

As against these disadvantages may be set off the ardour of industry in the small cultivator.

It is often said that though the gross produce of land is greatest under small cultivation, yet the net produce, *i.e.*, the surplus after feeding the cultivators, must be smaller and therefore can only maintain a small population engaged in other pursuits, such as commerce or the liberal professions. No doubt it may be true that the non-agricultural population will bear a smaller proportion to the agricultural under a system of small cultivation, because more of the latter are being supported, but it does not necessarily follow that the non-agricultural population will be *absolutely* less. The proportion may be 3 to 1 of agricultural to non-agricultural population in the case of a country where there is small farming, and 2 to 1 in a case where there is large farming, but supposing there to be equality of population or rather of the capacity of supporting a population, the $\frac{1}{4}$ that is non-agricultural in the former case may be actually greater than the $\frac{1}{3}$ which is non-agricultural in the latter. Of course there is a point when small holdings are so split up as to become tiny patches, or *parcelles*; then this argument holds good, because in such cases the farms become too small to be worked profitably at all.

15. The Laws of the Increase of the Productive Agents.

The laws of the increase of production depend on

    A. Labour.

    B. Capital.

    C. Land.

    A. Increase of labour = increase of population,

which tends to double itself in one generation unless restrained by

(i) Positive checks, *i.e.*, such as an individual cannot control, like earthquakes, famines, etc.

(ii) By preventative checks, *i.e.*, those due to prudence and self control, such as the custom in some countries that a girl should not marry until she had spun and woven for herself a trousseau sufficient for her whole subsequent life.

Thus impediments to the increase of production do not arise from A.

B. Capital = product of saving. Therefore increase of Capital depends on

(i) The amount of the fund from which saving can be made, *i.e.*, the surplus of the produce of labour after supplying the necessaries of life to all concerned in the production.

(ii) The strength of the dispositions which prompt it, *e.g.*, as a rule the greater the profit that can be made from Capital, the stronger is the motive to its accumulation; but gain is not only attended by external inducements, there is diversity in the effective strength of the desire of accumulation, caused by

(*a*) The element of uncertainty of life. Men in safe occupations put by more for the future than men in hazardous occupations, *e.g.*, sailors are notorious prodigals.

(*b*) Improvidence, arising from intellectual as well as moral causes: when things future do not act with any force on the imagination or will.

(*c*) Want of interest in others, *e.g.*, the men in the later Roman Empire cared nothing for their heirs.

Examples may be found both of (1) deficiency and of (2) excess in the strength of the desire of accumulation.

(1) Examples of deficiency are chiefly to be found in any backward stage of civilization, such as the hunting stage.

Cf. (*a*) The Indian villagers on the St. Lawrence will content themselves with clearing small patches for the growth of maize in the most fertile locality.

(*b*) This arises from defect of industry, but defect of providence is to be found, *e.g.*, among the Chinese, who are content with destructible houses and implements and expect a nominal 12% and an actual 18 to 36% on their Capital—a great contrast to Holland in its prosperous days, when men still continued to save Capital for a return of 2%.

(2) Examples of excesses are to be found

(*a*) In England (1848) owing to the long exemption of the country from the ravages of war, free political institutions, and the desire to rise in rank, aided by the English incapacity for personal enjoyment, but retarded by the desire to make a show, which has not affected

(*b*) Holland, where the disposition to save reached the highest point, and there were no idle rich to set the example of reckless expenditure.

The fact that there can be this excessive desire of accumulation shows that there is no necessary limitation to production in B any more than in A. Therefore it must be due to—

C. Land. *The limited quantity and limited productiveness of land set the real limit to production.*

This limit is not a fixed obstacle like a wall, but may be compared rather to an elastic band. The principle on which it works is known as the *law of diminishing return*, which is that in any given state of agricultural skill, by increasing the labour, the produce is not increased to an equal degree, or, in other words, every increase of produce is obtained by a more than proportional increase in the application of labour to the land. This is obvious when, in order to raise extra produce, it is necessary to have recourse to inferior land, for the very meaning of inferior land is land which, with equal labour, returns a smaller amount of produce. The inferiority may be either in fertility or in situation (*i.e.*, distance from the market), but the principle is the same if, instead of having recourse to inferior land, attempts are made by the application of more labour, more manure, etc., to make the same piece of land produce more. Thus the produce of land increases, *caeteris paribus*, in a diminishing ratio to the increase of the labour and Capital employed, but the law may be suspended or temporarily controlled by whatever adds to the general power of mankind over nature, and especially by an extension of their knowledge, and their consequent command, of the properties and powers of natural agents.

Such retarding factors are

(i) Improved processes of agriculture, *e.g.*, the introduction of the Swedish turnip, inventions like sub-soil draining.

(ii) Improved means of communication, *e.g.*, construction of railways which diminish the inferiority of distant lands.

(iii) Mechanical improvements which apparently have little to do with agriculture, *e.g.*, an improved process of smelting iron which diminishes the cost of railroads, buildings, etc.

(iv) Improvements in education; for the intelligence of the workman is a most important factor in the productiveness of labour.

N.B.—The law of diminishing return applies to all the arts which extract materials from the globe, *e.g.*, to mining no less than to agriculture, but in the case of a mine it acts more rapidly, for the time comes when the mine is actually exhausted; at the same time the retarding agency of improvements, etc., also applies in a still greater degree, for mining operations are more susceptible to mechanical improvements than agricultural.

16. Consequences of Foregoing Laws.

We have seen that a *possible* limit to production lies in a deficiency of the desire to accumulate Capital and a *certain* limit in the operation of the law of diminishing return in regard to land. What are the remedies for these two limitations?

A. The remedies when the limit to Production is the weakness of the principle of accumulation are

(i) A better Government, such as gives complete security of property, better tenure of land, moderate and equitable taxes, etc.

(ii) Education.

(iii) The introduction of foreign arts and the importation of foreign Capital which, besides allowing for increased production independently of the thrift of the inhabitants themselves, sets a stimulating example before them.

B. The limit caused by the operation of the law of diminishing returns can only be set back by restraining the population. Such necessity for restraint is not confined to a state of inequality of property, though this may cause it to be earlier felt. The niggardliness of nature, not the injustice of Society, is the cause of the penalty attached to over-population. It is in vain to say that all mouths which the increase of mankind calls into existence bring with them hands. The new mouths require as much food as the old ones, and the hands do not produce as much. Everywhere, and at all times, there is, as it were, a race between the growth of population and the progress of improvement, and when the former outstrips the latter recourse has to be had to two expedients—

(i) The importation of food from abroad. This, like any other improvement, throws back the decline of the productive power of labour by a certain distance, but it cannot stay it for ever, for

(*a*) The available corn growing regions do not comprise the whole globe, and even all the corn growing regions are not available, by reason of difficulties of communication which can only slowly be overcome.

(*b*) Even from that small part of the surface of the countries which export corn, only a limited quantity of food can be drawn without an increase of the proportional cost, because in such of those countries as exhibit a strong effective desire of accumulation there will probably also be a rapidly increasing population, and their agriculture has to provide for their own expanding numbers (*e.g.*, United States); while in those where the desire is weak there are obvious difficulties in raising the Capital for the production of the surplus corn for export, and foreign capital is not always easily imported, owing to differences of language, manners, etc. (*e.g.*, Russia).

(ii) Emigration. Of this the efficacy is real in so far as it consists in seeking elsewhere tracts of fertile land which, if they existed at home, would enable the demand of an increasing population to be met, and it is quite effectual when the region to be colonised is near at hand, but it is difficult to believe that a permanent stream of emigration to distant countries sufficient to take off all the excessive increase of a population can be kept up.

17. The Distribution of Wealth.

We have seen that the laws and conditions of the production of Wealth partake of the character of physical truths. There is nothing optional or arbitrary in them, and though we may succeed by increased knowledge in making for ourselves more space within the limits set by the constitution of things, we know there must be a limit and cannot alter the ultimate properties either of matter or mind, but the distribution of Wealth *is a matter of human institution solely*. The things once there, mankind, individually or collectively, can do with them as they like. The laws of Distribution therefore are the laws and customs of Society, which are determined by the opinions and feelings of the ruling portion of the community. We have to consider, not the causes, but the consequences, of the rules according to which Wealth may be distributed, and these consequences have as much the character of physical laws as the laws of Production, for though human beings can control their own acts, they cannot control the consequences of those acts, either to themselves or to others. What, then, are the different modes of distributing the produce of land and labour which have been adopted in practice, or may be conceived in theory?

18. The Institution of Property and Rival Systems.

The institution of private property came about through the giving of legal effect to first occupancy in order to preserve the peace, but in order to consider the Institution properly it must not be regarded only as having this primitive origin, but also as a possible institution of later growth, when it is to be presumed that the initial appropriation to private persons would be accompanied by none of the inequalities and injustices which mark the principle in old Societies, but the division of goods once made would not again be interfered with : individuals would be left to their own exertions. Now there have been Societies on a small scale, *e.g.*, the Monastic orders, the Moravians, etc., which have excluded individual property and adopted a plan of common ownership, while the theorists who have assailed individal property have been more numerous than those who have actually adopted any rival scheme. They are of two classes—

A. Those who would distribute all the physical means of life with absolute equality (Communism).

B. Those who admit inequality but would attempt to ground it on some principle—justice or general expediency, and not on accident alone, while at the same time requiring that the land and instruments of production should be the property, not of individuals, but of Communities or of the Government (St. Simonism and Fourierism).

N.B.—The general term for both A and B is Socialism.

A. Communism as advocated by Owen and Louis Blanc. The chief objections to this substitute for private property are—

(i) Under such a system each person will be chiefly occupied in evading his fair share of work.

Con. — This argument pre-supposes that honest work is only to be had from those who individually reap the benefit of their own exertions, but this is not an advantage of the present system of private property, and the argument cannot be used for those working for a wage, like the Irish reaper, or those working for a fixed salary, like the Chief Justice. The substitute for the "master's eye" under a Communist system is the eye of the whole community. The worker under a Communist system would have a public motive and be under the compulsion of public opinion, but whether there would be greater or less energy of labour under Communism is at present (1852) undecided.

(ii) If all members of a community were assured of a livelihood, there would be no prudential restraint on the multiplication of mankind.

Con.—Surely Communism provides motives to restraint equivalent to those which it would take away, for it would immediately become obvious under Communism that any great increase of the population diminished the comfort of the whole community, and public opinion would soon take steps to remove the danger of over-population.

(iii) A more real difficulty is that of fairly apportioning the labour of the community among its members. How is anyone to find out what each individual is fit for? And if you overcome this difficulty by making everyone do each kind of work in turn, you sacrifice the advantages of a co-operative production.

Con.—These are real but not necessarily insuperable difficulties. Human intelligence guided by a sense of justice ought to be able to find a way of apportioning work at any rate with less inequality and injustice than under the present system.

Thus Communism appears to have advantages over the existing state of affairs, but in order to be just in the comparison between Communism and Private Property one should compare Communism at its best with the institution of property, not as it is, but as it might be. As it is in modern Europe, it rests on conquests and violence; its laws conform to none of the principles on which the system rests, and they foster inequalities in the race of life. Thus Private Property is supposed to guarantee to individuals the fruits of *their own* labour and abstinence, and when it gives people (*e.g.*, by bequest) the fruits of the labour of others, a consequence arises which actually conflicts with the ends which render the institution legitimate; bnt suppose everything inequitable under the present system removed, and suppose both Communism and Private Property to be tried in conjunction with universal education and a due limitation of the numbers of the community, *i.e.*, suppose both systems were tried under the most favourable conditions, which is likely to be superior? The answer will probably depend on which of the two systems is consistent with the greatest amount of human liberty. After *subsistence* is assured, man wants *liberty*, and we may probably add to the objections to Communism—

(iv) That it would leave no room for individuality of character.

B. The other forms of Socialism mainly differ from Communism by retaining the incentives to labour derived from private pecuniary interest. They are—

(1) *St. Simonism.* Under this scheme a ruling body would arrange all men in grades, like a regiment, and there would be different pay in the different grades. Such a system might work well where you had a body of men like the Jesuits in Paraguay, obviously fitted by their marked superiority to the rest to do the work of the ruling body, but whether such an arrangement would work for long, even under the best conditions, or would be tolerated at all where there was not this marked difference between the rulers and the ruled is open to doubt. Men will acquiesce in a fixed rule like that of equality, or in chance and external necessity, but would certainly not submit to a handful of human beings weighing everybody in the balance and giving more to one and less to another at their sole judgment.

(2) *Fourierism.* This system does not abolish private property nor even inheritance. It organises industry into associations of about 2,000 members, which are under the guidance of chiefs selected by themselves. In the distribution a minimum is assigned for the subsistance of every member, while the remainder is shared in predetermined proportions among the three elements, Labour, Capital and Talent. The share appor-

tioned to Talent is estimated by a person's grade, to which he is elected by his companions. Separate *ménages* are allowed, but all have to live in the same pile of buildings, to save expense both in building and in other branches of domestic economy.

The Fourierists claim, by an argument based on the fact that men will undergo severe exertions for the sake of pleasure, that they have solved the problem of rendering labour attractive, but they forget that it is a very different thing being compelled to do a thing from being able to do it or not as you like. It certainly seems as if this system does no very great violence to any of the general laws by which human action even at present is influenced, and is worth a trial; but on the whole the political economist at the present moment must be most concerned with the conditions of a society founded on private property and individual competition, and with discovering how the present system can be improved.

[Mill's views on Socialism passed through many stages. In the first edition of "The Principles" (1848) he found the arguments against Communism conclusive, and the assumption on which St. Simonism rested almost too chimerical to be reasoned against. Fourierism he did not discuss at all. The more favourable view analysed above is taken from an edition of 1852. In 1869 he planned a book on Socialism, the rough drafts of which were published after his death in the form of articles, and from this we gather that he then regarded the Socialist attack on the present competitive system as argumentatively unjust, because the main evils exposed might be remedied without destroying the system; he also criticised the main constructive proposals of the Socialists chiefly on the grounds that a training would be necessary to make men morally fitted for them, and that, especially in a scheme which would nationalise the whole productive resources of a country, the difficulty of management would be too great.]

19. Analysis of the Institution of Property.

A. What is essential to the institution of property?

(i) Freedom of *acquisition by contract*. In other words, under the institution a man not only has the right to what he himself produces, an object which it is hard to identify when there are many parties to an act of production, but also the right to what has been produced by others if obtained by their free consent.

(ii) The validity of *prescription*. After a thing has been held for a certain length of time, however wrongfully possession was originally obtained of it, more wrong is generally done by the dispossession of the present owner than by leaving the original wrong without atonement.

(iii) The power of *bequest*. It arises naturally out of the idea of property that a man should have the power of leaving it after he is dead as he chooses.

B. Things that are not essential to the idea of property.

(i) The right of *inheritance* as distinguished from bequest. It may be a proper arrangement that the property of an intestate man should pass first to his children and then to his nearest relations, but it is by no means a necessary result of the principle of private property. Inheritance is a natural arrangement, indeed the only arrangement, in the primitive state of society when the maintenance of the unit of the family was so important that even bequest was seldom recognised, but the unit of Society is now no longer the family but the individual, and property is now inherent in individuals, and not in families.

Now there is something to say for the State seeing that the children of an intestate are provided for out of his estate in such a way as they should have been had he lived, but collateral relatives stand in quite a different position; no one would recognise their claims at all if the State did not recognise them. Children are in a different position, but it cannot be maintained that a father owes the whole of a fortune he has acquired to his child, apart from the fact that it is probably bad for the latter to become the possessor of so much unearned wealth. The obvious duty of a parent towards a human being whose existence he has caused is to see that he starts life with such appliances as to give him a fair chance of achieving success. What is fair in the matter is to be found in the law regulating the provision to be made for illegitimate children and in the usual treatment meted out to the younger children of the nobility and landed gentry.

(ii) Possible *limitations in* the power of *bequest* itself—which may be so exercised as to conflict with the permanent interests of the human race, *e.g.*, when a gift is tied up for perpetuity, or when property left for public uses is left on conditions that bind for perpetuity. Such are obvious limitations, but Roman law, after it permitted bequest at all, insisted that fixed portions should be reserved for each child, and France in following this law makes the extreme restriction that each child must share alike, and that a man can bequeath by will only a part equal to the share of each child, a restriction adopted as a democratic expedient to break down primogeniture and the accumulation of wealth in large masses. Perhaps the better way to make such restrictions would be not to restrict what each man might bequeath, but what anyone should be permitted to acquire.

(iii) Ought exclusive ownership to be recognised in *land* which is not the produce of the owner's labour, nor accumulated by abstinence?

Exclusive use would certainly have to be given for a period, for the person who ploughs and sows must be permitted to reap, and where, if not the land, at any rate most of its valuable qualities are the produce of industry (cf. the Bedford Level), there is an economic justification for private property in it, but this is only when the proprietor is the improver of the land, which is not always the case in Great Britain (1848) where the heir who gets the land frequently gets too little personal property to support it, where leases to farmers are frequently refused, and where such leases as are granted contain restrictive covenants.

Now landed property is felt even by those most tenacious of its rights to be a different thing from other property; hence in all countries obligations are attached to the owners of land, either morally or legally, and it is but a step from regarding the possessors of land as public functionaries to discarding them altogether. If discarded, they should be compensated according to the general principles on which property rests, *i.e.*, either on the ground that the land was bought with the labour of produce and abstinence, or on the ground of prescription. At any rate, if any man is allowed an exclusive right over a portion of the common inheritance of the land, it should be seen to it not merely as in the case of personal property that no evil is done, but that it is productive of positive good, and the general public should not be deprived of rights like rights of access which do not damage the produce. The species at large still retains all its original claim to the soil of the planet which it inhabits as much as is compatible with the purposes for which it has parted with the remainder.

(iv) The civilised world is gradually making up its mind against property in anything else other than in the produce of labour, or in land, *e.g.*, property in human beings (though when such property is recognised, compensation must be paid for abolishing it. Compare " that great measure of Justice of 1833 "). Other examples of property in abuses are property in commissions in the Army, in advowson, in the right of following certain trades or professions, etc., etc. In all these cases compensation should be paid on abolition if they have acquired the character of permanent property by prescription.

20. Classes who divide the Produce.

A. Speaking generally, Produce is to be divided into three shares which remunerate—

(i) The owner of the land.

(ii) The owner of the capital.

(iii) The productive labourer.

All the rest of the population, whether giving any services or not, is supported at the expense of these three classes.

B. Sometimes the three are united in one, a case which embraces the two extremes of existing society in respect to the independence and dignity of the labouring classes, for the cases are—

(i) Where the labourer owns the land and either owns or at any rate employs the capital himself (*i.e.*, peasant proprietorship).

(ii) Where the landowner owns the labourer as well as the capital (*i.e.*, slavery).

C. The owners of two of the three requisites of production are often united in one person, *e.g.*:

(i) The same person owns the capital and land but not the labour, the labourers being neither serfs on the one hand nor proprietors on the other (*e.g.*, Metayer System).

(ii) The labourer may own stock on the land, but not the land itself, a system which prevails in Ireland (1848) and in India (*e.g.*, Cottier and Ryot Tenure).

21. Competition v. Custom.

Political economists usually speak as if competition alone were the only determining agency in dividing the produce, and as if it effected all that it has a tendency to do. Monopolies and the interference of authority with the operation of competition are allowed for, but little allowance is made for another agency that often supplants competition altogether, *i.e.*, custom. It is well to understand once and for all the extent to which custom interferes with competition, because succeeding arguments will assume the unhampered operation of competition, and therefore these observations must be used as a general correction, to be applied whenever relevant. Custom is older than competition. It is the first barrier erected between the weak and the strong, at a time when there are no laws or Government able to protect the weak or to safeguard free competition. The operation of custom is particularly seen in the following cases:—

(i) The relations between the landowner and the cultivator. In these we generally find the payment made by the latter to the former is not regulated by competition, but is determined by the usage of the country, and that a holder of land acquires as a rule fixity of tenure on condition of his paying his customary rent, *e.g.*,

(*a*) The Ryot or peasant farmer of India who has usually held his land from time immemorial, and is thought entitled to retain it as long as the customary rent is paid to the Government.

(*b*) In Europe the characteristic land tenure is that arising from the assignment of land to a serf who has to do fixed work on the lands of his lord. By degrees these obligations became definite, and, later, payments in money were substituted for them. Custom enforced these changes at every stage, and custom, too, was responsible for the final result—a class of free tenantry who held their land in perpetuity on fixed conditions.

(*c*) Where the original holdings did not arise from personal bondage, there often grew up in Europe a system called the *Metayer*, under which the landlord, who generally supplies the stock, receives instead of land and profit a fixed proportion of the produce. This proportion, whether two-thirds or a half, is a fixed one, not variable from farm to farm, or from tenant to tenant.

(ii) In retail trade prices are sometimes unaffected by competition. It is often said that there cannot be two prices in the same market. So competition ordains, but custom says otherwise. In retail trade in almost every town there are cheap shops and dear shops selling the same articles, and the same shop often sells the same article at different prices to different customers, though competition, owing to rapidity of transport and the growth of large businesses, is tending to drive out custom in retail, as it has already driven it out in wholesale, trade.

(iii) In nearly all professional remuneration, *e.g.*, fees of doctors and lawyers, competition does not lower the fees themselves but only diminishes each competitor's chance of obtaining them.

22. Economical Relations not affected by Competition.

A. Slavery, the result of brute force.
B. Peasant Proprietorship. ⎫
C. The Metayer System. ⎬ Produced by Custom.

A. *Slavery.* In this system all the produce belongs to the landlord; the labourers possess nothing but what he thinks fit to give them, and their wretchedness is only limited by his humanity or his pecuniary interest which, when slaves are easily obtainable, is often best served by working those he has to death. If a fresh supply is not easily got, his interest suggests keeping up the number by breeding, which necessitates a far better treatment of them : hence the comparatively good condition of slaves in the ancient world.

Slave labour is not good economically for the following reasons :—

(i) Labour extorted by fear of punishment is inefficient and unproductive, though perhaps human beings may be driven by the lash to do things which they would not do freely, *e.g.*, work on sugar plantations in America.

(ii) Slavery brutifies the intellect and therefore

cannot be used for products which require much skill.

(iii) Even the animal strength of the slave is usually not half exerted, *e.g.*, two Middlesex mowers will mow in a day as much grass as six Russian serfs.

(iv) Direction and superintendence are usually bad, because the landed proprietors in such a system are the only guides and directors of the industry.

There can be no intermediate class of capitalist farmers, and great landowners are everywhere an idle class, or if they labour at all addict themselves only to the more exciting kinds of exercise.

N.B.—It does not necessarily follow because free labour would be better for the community than slave labour that the emancipation of their slaves would benefit the proprietors. This depends upon the wages of free labour in the particular place, and that in turn on the growth of the population. The maintenance of slaves or serfs may become a too costly matter, and it might pay the proprietors to be free of them (*e.g.*, if the Irish peasantry were slaves, 1848), but where the soil is rich and under-peopled the balance of profit is probably on the side of slavery (*e.g.*, West Indies, where slave owners probably did not get compensation equal to their loss), but slavery is a cause completely judged and decided in spite of the extraordinary sympathy shown in Great Britain with the Southern States of America (1865).

No European country, except Spain alone, any longer participates in the enormity. England's example was followed first by Denmark, then by the provisional Government of France, and not long after by the Dutch.

B. *Peasant Proprietorship.* Here the distinction of rent, profits and wages does not exist. They all go into the same hands. Which is best, small properties in land, or large?

(i) On the Continent the benefit of having a numerous proprietory population is almost universally taken for granted.

(ii) English people for the most part favour large properties, holding that people on the Continent are unaware of the advantages of a great accumulation of capital on large farms, to which it may be answered that the English are now unacquainted with the advantages of peasant proprietorship, which once gave them their gallant yoemen, and of which the only example left in England is the statesmen of Cumberland and Westmoreland, the originals of Wordsworth's "Peasantry." Therefore it is important for English people to study the testimony of observers to the advantages of peasant proprietorship in various countries—

(*a*) In Switzerland the evidence of Sismondi and Inglis is to the following effect:—

The industry, security and confidence in the future, etc., of the Swiss peasantry is remarkable. It must be pointed out, however, that nearly all the properties are mortgaged, but seldom to more than half their registered value. Again, in some of the cantons, the land is so sub-divided that the proprietors often find it hard to support themselves on their small estates. However, so great has been the improvement in agriculture since the sub-division of the feudal estates into peasant properties that it is not uncommon (*e.g.*, Thürgau) for $\frac{1}{3}$ or $\frac{1}{4}$ part of an estate to produce as much grain and support as many head of cattle as the whole estate did before.

(*b*) In Norway. Laing points out, besides the beneficial effects of proprietorship as in Switzerland, the habit of co-operation among the Norwegian peasant proprietors, especially in the matter of irrigation, water being brought down from the heads of the glens in wooden troughs which are sometimes continued for forty miles. The same observer also points out that such improvements in agriculture as large farms are beginning to adopt, *e.g.*, furrow draining, stall feeding in summer, liquid manures, etc., have been in use among the peasant proprietors of Switzerland, Norway, etc., for generations.

(*c*) In Germany. Howitt says the peasant proprietors of the Palatinate are probably the most industrious peasantry in the world. They are slow but for ever doing. They plod on from day to day and from year to year, the most patient, untirable and persevering of animals. The English peasant is so cut off from the idea of property that he comes to look upon it as a thing off which he is warned by the laws of the large proprietors, and becomes in consequence spiritless and purposeless. Other writers bear testimony to the skill and intelligence of this peasantry, their judicious employment of manures and excellent rotation of crops.

Kay says of Saxony that since the peasants became proprietors of the land there has been a rapid and continuous improvement in the condition of the houses, the manner of living, the dress of the peasants and particularly in the culture of the land. He notes also the willingness of the peasants to send their children to agricultural schools.

(*d*) In Belgium. The soil of Belgium was originally one of the worst in Europe, but McCullock points out that the industry of the Flemish proprietor is gradually improving in a way that makes it surpass the most improved soil in Britain, and there is so much competition for small farms that land pays little more than 2 % on purchase money.

A great deal of distress was caused in 1846-7 by partial failure of all kinds of grain and an almost total one of potato, and some hold that it was especially severe in Flanders owing to the large number of the population directly dependent on the soil, but the distress was severe everywhere, and probably the Flemish peasant did not suffer so much as the English day labourer.

(*e*) In the Channel Islands. Various writers point out the prosperity and happiness of these islands, where the average sized farm is under 16 acres, and were quite inferior land fetches about £4 per acre in rent.

(*f*) In France. It is from France that the impressions unfavourable to peasant proprietors are chiefly drawn, the chief argument being that the sub-division of the land is rapidly reducing the peasantry to the verge of starvation. Arthur Young, who travelled in France just before the Revolution and who had been the introducer of large farming in England, felt compelled to testify to the remarkable excellence of cultivation where peasant proprietorship existed. It is of such lands that he says "the magic of property turns sand to gold," and again, "give a man the secure position of a bleak rock and he will turn it into a garden. Give him a nine years' lease of a garden and he will convert it into a desert." He, however, points out that where the properties are too small the agriculture is bad, and recommends that a limit to sub-division should be fixed by law.

Thus there can be no doubt of the good influence of peasant properties (*a*) in stimulating industry, and (*b*) in training intelligence, but (*c*) what is the effect on that most important problem respecting the condition of the labouring classes, the problem of population? On this point there is discrepancy of experience which can be accounted for by the fact that labouring people, whether they live by land or by wages, have always hitherto multiplied up to the limit set by their habitual standard of comfort, but are peasant proprietors more or less likely to do this than hired labourers? Probably less. The dependence of wages on population is a matter of speculation, but every peasant can satisfy himself as to how many persons his piece of land can support, and the balance of the evidence from the writers whose observations are summarised above serves to show that population under peasant proprietors tends to keep just below the point that would produce a sub-division into farms that would barely support human existence. The experience of France most decidedly contradicts the asserted tendency of peasant proprietorship to produce excess of population, and there is no single authentic instance which supports the assertion that rapid multiplication is promoted by peasant properties, though instances may certainly be cited to show that it is not prevented by them. Even where there is excess of numbers it does not follow that there is too great sub-division of the land. Just as large properties are perfectly compatible with small farms, so are small properties with farms of adequate size. In many places where several children inherit a small estate they prefer to sell it entire and share the proceeds rather than divide it up. There are certainly some parts of Germany and France where *morcellement* or the excessive splitting up of estates is an evil, but it is diminishing and not increasing, and it is brought about rather by the high price that can be made by selling land to the peasantry, than by any inherent vice in peasant proprietorship itself.

23. Two-fold Division of the Produce.

A. *The Metayer System* is the chief example of a case when the division of the produce between two parties (*i.e.*, the labourer and the landlord) is fixed by *custom*. The proportion is usually $\frac{1}{2}$, but in some parts of Italy it is $\frac{2}{3}$; and there is great divergence of local custom as to the amount of the capital supplied by the landlord, sometimes it is the whole and sometimes certain parts, *e.g.*, the cattle and seed.

>(i) The *advantages* of the Metayer system lie in the same direction as those of peasant proprietorship, *i.e.*, (*a*) in stimulating industry, (*b*) in training intelligence and (*c*) in promoting forethought and self-

> control—but to rather a less degree because the Metayers have only half the interest. Still the same reasons operate to promote prudence in the matter of increasing the population, and there is an additional reason preventing sub-division in the Metayer system, viz., that the landlord may exercise a controlling power.

The evidence from Italy is very favourable to the system and points to considerable prosperity among the Metayers.

> (ii) The characteristic *disadvantage* of the Metayer system is that the Metayer has no interest in putting any of his profits into the improvement of the land. It might be the interest of a Metayer to make the land produce as much as could be brought out of it by means of the stock furnished by the proprietor, but it could never be his interest to mix any part of his own stock with it.
>
> English authorities from Arthur Young downwards utterly condemn the Metayer system, but it must be remembered that their impressions are chiefly derived from France, and from France before the Revolution, when the Metayers paid all the taxes, which were extremely heavy. Nor had the French Metayers the fixity of tenure of the Metayers of Italy; so, as they could call nothing their own and could not in any contingency be worse off, they had nothing to restrain them from multiplying and sub-dividing the land until stopped by actual starvation.

Thus the Metayer system need not necessarily be a bad one, and if it is to be got rid of, it should be got rid of, not by putting farmers into the place of Metayers, but by transforming the existing Metayers into farmers by ridding them of the landlord's claim to half the produce and letting them pay in lieu of it a moderate fixed rent, though perhaps the effect of this would be for the Metayer to lose his Capitalist partner, for the landowner would probably no longer consent to imperil his movable property on the hazards of agricultural enterprise when sure of a fixed money income without it. Of course if the Metayer were converted into a mere tenant at the will of the landlord, he would be much worse off than before.

24. Two-fold Division of the Produce.

B. *Cottier Tenancy* = all cases in which the labourer makes his contract for land without the intervention of a Capitalist farmer, and in which the amount of rent, etc., is determined, not by custom, but by *competition*. Ireland (1848) provides the chief example of this form of tenure.

(i) *Nature of the tenure.* The produce is divided into two portions—rent, and the remuneration of the labourer—and the one is evidently determined by the other, while the rent being determined by competition evidently depends upon the demand for land and the supply of it, and the demand depends on the number of the competitors, who are the whole rural population. Thus in this tenure the principal of population acts directly on the land, not, as in England, on Capital. Unless something checks the increase of population, the competition for land forces up rent to the highest point consistent with keeping population alive. Now rents might be kept down by a high standard of comfort among the people and a moderate increase of numbers, but even then Cottier tenants having no fixity of tenure would be disinclined to improve their lands for fear of having their rents raised. It is only when some such custom as the Ulster Tenant Right (by which outgoing tenants obtain considerable sums from their successors for the goodwill of their farms) limits competition that any safeguard is provided for permanence of tenure.

(ii) *Consequences of Cottier tenancy.* Where the amount of rent is not limited, either by law or custom, the Cottier system has the disadvantages of the worst Metayer system, with scarcely any of the advantages by which the Metayers are compensated.

(*a*) The system of Agriculture is almost sure to be bad.

(*b*) The motives to prudence are weaker than in the case of the Metayers when they are protected by custom from losing their farms. With an over-populated country the competition for farms is so high that the rents are often forced up to nine times the value of the land. It is likely that those rents will become merely nominal and that the result will be habits of recklessness in the tenant, for if the landlord exerted his full rights the Cottier would be unable to live, and if he were industrious, frugal and prudent, he would only have more to pay his landlord. It is usual to ascribe the want of energy in the Irish people in improving their condition to a peculiar indolence in the Celtic race, but it has really been the result of their system of land tenure. No labourers work harder in England or America than the Irish, but not under a Cottier system.

(The Ryot tenancy of India resembles the Cottier system in having only two contracting parties, but the landlord in India is generally the sovereign, and therefore rents have the nature of taxes, and these payments have generally been fixed by *custom*. The English made the mistake at first of treating the collectors of these rents, the Zemindars, as if they were the landowners and not merely tax collectors, as they really were, and they practically endowed a useless body of great landlords from the public revenue. These new landlords ruined their estates and themselves, and the English did not make a similar mistake in the later provinces added to the Empire: Government itself became the direct landlord, generally giving the cultivators comparative security of tenure, at rents fixed as far as possible according to their ability to pay).

(iii) *Means of abolishing Cottier Tenancy.* The potato famine of 1848 forced the English Government to pay some attention to the Irish agrarian problem, but it did not realise that the very foundation of the economical evils of Ireland was due to the Cottier system. Ireland under Cottier agriculture could no longer supply food to its population. Parliament by way of remedy applied a stimulus to population but none at all to production. The situation was only saved by the Wakefield system of self-supporting emigration, which helped to produce a diminution in population of a million and a-half between 1841 and 1851 [by 1871 the population had diminished by nearly three millions], but it is no real solution of the problem to drive people off the land of their own country. The paramount consideration is by what mode of appropriation and cultivation it may be made most useful to the collective body of its inhabitants. Various proposals have been made for dealing with the situation, viz. :—

(*a*) Transforming the Cottiers into hired labourers. This might improve Irish agriculture, but how would it improve the Irish people? The situation would remain the same as far as they were concerned.

(*b*) Giving long leases. This is no remedy (as the experience of Ireland shows) where rents are fixed by competition at a higher amount than can be paid. It acts better in India where the Government, being itself the landlord, can fix the rent according to its own judgment.

(*c*) Giving perpetuity or fixity of tenure, *i.e.*, changing the rent into a quit-rent and the farmer into a peasant proprietor.

This could be done in the case of Ireland by fixing the rents at those now actually paid, not the nominal rents, and giving the landlords a compensation for the present value of the chances of increase in their rents. This would of course expropriate the higher classes of Ireland, a justifiable act if the sole means of effecting a great public good. It would also leave none but peasant proprietors, which would perhaps be a bad thing for agriculture, because large farms are useful for experiment, etc.

(*d*) Allowing anyone who reclaims waste land to become the owner of it at a fixed quit-rent—of course making the surrender of such waste lands compulsory on the landlords.

(*e*) Buying through societies formed for the purpose as much as possible of the land offered for sale, and selling it again in small portions as peasant properties.

[*Subsequent history of the Irish Land Question*. The somehat disproportionate space that Mill devotes to Irish land tenure was due to the fact that the First Edition of the *Principles* (1848) was produced at a time when Irish affairs were forced into prominence by the great famine of 1846. When Mill produced his last edition in 1865 he noticed in Ireland a tendency on the one hand for small holdings to disappear in favour of those of a medium size, and on the other the germs of a tendency to the formation of peasant proprietorships which required only the aid of a friendly legislator for the cost of them. In 1870 an Irish Land Act was passed which, accepting the principle of dual ownership, gave tenants the right of compensation for disturbance. Gladstone's Act of 1881 attempted to establish the three "F's" (fair rents, free sale of tenants interests and fixed tenures) but it was not until 1903, when the Act known as "Wyndham's Act" was passed, giving an opportunity to tenants to acquire their own lands from the landlords on terms satisfactory to both parties, that the real foundation of Peasant Proprietorship in Ireland was laid, and what Mill hoped for was at length realised].

25. The Three-fold Division of the Produce. (I) Wages.

A. *General Theory of Wages.* Wages depend on the proportion between the number of the labouring population and that part of circulating Capital which is devoted to the purchase of labour, together with all funds which are paid in exchange for unproductive labour (and therefore are not Capital). The two sources may be together called the Wages Fund.

[The Wages Fund theory here enunciated was afterwards abandoned by Mill himself. Such a doctrine could only have arisen in a country like England where, in practice, wages are *paid out of* Capital, but even here it does not follow that they are *determined by* Capital.]

Three popular theories regarding wages need to be considered:—

(i) That wages are high when trade is good. Now it is true that when the demand for any commodity is brisk, the demand for labour in that employment is more pressing and higher wages are paid, and that the contrary is the case when there is a stagnation. This is a complication obscuring the operation of general causes. It must be remembered that Capital which the manufacturer does not employ, or which is locked up in unsold goods, is, as far as the labourer is concerned, Capital which does not exist.

(ii) That high prices make high wages. Brisk demand which causes temporary high prices causes also temporary high wages. High prices might also induce dealers to save more Capital for the Wages Fund. This might be the case if the high prices came from Heaven or from abroad, because Capital would be increased by them, but if they are the result of restrictive laws and fall on the remaining members of the community, they can only benefit one set of labourers at the expense of others, because all the people who pay the high prices have their means of saving reduced.

(iii) That wages (*i.e.*, money wages) vary with

the price of food, rising when it rises and falling when it falls. If the dearness or cheapness of food is temporary, it probably does not affect wages at all except in a contrary direction to this, because in times of scarcity labourers compete more violently for employment, and so cause a fall in wages, but when the dearness or cheapness is of a permanent character it may affect wages, but only through the operation of the law of wages, *i.e.*, by affecting the population, for when food is dear a greater number of the children will prematurely die, or if the standard of comfort among the labouring classes is high enough, a rise in prices might be an additional restraint on multiplication. In these cases wages would adapt themselves to the price of food, though after an interval of almost a generation. The question is, is there a minimum rate of wages as Ricardo assumed? Abstractly there might be, but in practice the minimum itself is likely to vary. If an obstacle to the lowering of wages is a high standard of comfort among the labourers, a rise in the price of food would gradually effect either a prudential check to population, or a lowering of the standard of comfort. The same laws operate conversely when the price of food is cheapened, *e.g.*, by the repeal of corn laws: then wages will gradually fall unless meanwhile a a higher standard of comfort has been set up which operates to check population, but this is not likely to be the case, because cheap food usually means more children surviving and earlier marriages.

Thus, excepting in the peculiar case of a new colony or in a particular trade from an extraordinarily rapid growth of capital employed in its occupation, high wages imply restraints on population. The population in few countries increases to its full extent, and the agency by which it is limited is, in the language of Malthus, preventive, not positive, *i.e.*, due to prudence, not to famine or disease. These preventive limits are in some cases legal (as where military service delays marriage), and in some cases the effect of peculiar customs. Such retarding customs in England were largely destroyed by the Poor Laws, which enabled the farmer to cast his labourers on parish pay, and in England there is now scarcely a relic of these indirect checks to population. So in the case of the common agricultural labourer the checks to population may almost be considered as non-existent, and sentimental objections to Malthusianism prevent people from testing the facts of the case, which amount to this, that *a due restriction of population is the only safeguard of the labouring class.* [Note the strong influence the teaching of Malthus had on Mill's theories.]

B. *The Remedies for Low Wages* :—

(i) *A minimum of wages* whether fixed by law or custom, with a guarantee of employment. This would imply a forced increase of the Wages Fund and the proportion between labour and the Wages Fund would thus be modified to the advantage of the labourers, not by restriction of population but by an increase of Capital.

Such a plan might be successful if it could be limited to the existing generation, but if those who have produced and accumulated are called upon to abstain from consuming until they have given food and clothing, not only to those who now exist but to all their descendants, all checks to the increase of population, both positive and preventive, would be suspended, and therefore this remedy would require as a condition legal measures for the repression of population.

It is for the same reason that Poor Law relief has to be accompanied with some conditions which people dislike. If there were no such conditions, the Poor Rate instituted by the famous Act of Elizabeth (1601) would by this time have absorbed the whole net produce of the land and labour of the country.

[The recent Trade Board's Act has adopted a minimum wage with regard to certain sweated industries, and it has in a short time very largely increased the wages in those industries without apparently causing any diminution of employment, but it has not yet been in existence long enough to judge what effect it will have on the next generation.]

(ii) *Allowances in aid of Wages.* This was an expedient resorted to for thirty years or so previous to 1834. This system as followed offered direct encouragement to population by giving relief in proportion to the number in the family. This need not be the method adopted, but even if it is not, the system has all the disadvantages common to all attempts to regulate wages without regulating population, and also a peculiar one of its own, viz., that when relief is given by the parish, employers will reduce the wages till the sum total of wages is as low as the wages were before. All that the allowance system does is to enable farmers to throw part of the support of their labourers upon the other inhabitants of the parish.

(iii) *The Allotment System.* This is another contrivance to compensate the labourer for the insufficiency of his wages by giving him something else as a supplement to them, *i.e.*, allowing him to rent a small piece of ground. The system has these advantages over the Allowance System that, instead of eking out insufficient wages by a fund raised from taxation, it does so by means which add to the gross produce of the country, and also instead of subsidising the labourer by a method that tends to make him idle it helps him by means of his own industry, but it is no better than the Allowance System in its effect on wages and population, and in spite of all precautions against Cottierism in the system it is, in essentials, neither more nor less than a system of Conacre [*i.e.*, the payment of wages in land]. The best that can be said for allotments is that they make the people grow their own poor rates.

These popular remedies do not touch the real root of the question, viz., the curbing of population, and no remedies have the smallest chance of being efficacious which do not operate on and through the minds and habits of the people. Unfortunately public opinion has taken a pernicious direction on the subject of population (*e.g.*, the teaching of the Roman Catholic Clergy): while a man who is intemperate in drink is discountenanced and despised by all who profess to be moral people, it is one of the chief grounds made use of in appeals to the benevolent that the applicant has a large family and is unable to maintain them.

A change would soon take place in the habits of the labouring classes if they were made to realise that the competition of too great numbers was the special cause of their poverty. The theory is familiar to all Trades Unions, for every successful combination to keep up wages owes its success to contrivances for restricting the number of competitors, and what is true of one employment is equally true of the general mass of employment.

Therefore to alter the habits of the labouring people there is need of—

> (iv) A two-fold action directed simultaneously upon their intelligence and their poverty, the first part being an effective system of *national education*, and the second, large measures of immediate relief through foreign and home *colonisation*. The foreign colonisation should be effected by a grant of money sufficient to establish in the colonies a considerable fraction of the youthful agricultural population, and the home colonisation should be effected by devoting all common land hereafter brought into cultivation to raising a class of small proprietors.
>
> [Mill himself acknowledged in his last edition the increase of emigration which rendered State aided emigration less necessary, and attempts have been made since his time, though with only partial success, to increase the number of small holdings.]

C. *The Difference of Wages in different Employments.* So far we have considered the causes which operate on wages generally, *i.e.*, the laws which govern the remuneration of average labour. We have now to consider how it is there is difference of wages in different employments. The causes of these differences have been analysed with tolerable success by Adam Smith (*Wealth of Nations*, Book I, Chap. 10), though his numerous examples are sometimes drawn from a state of affairs now no longer existing.

The main causes of differences may be summarised as follows:—

(i) *Different degrees of attractiveness* in different employments, such as their agreeableness or disagreeableness, the easiness and cheapness or difficulty and expense of learning them, of the probability or the improbability of success in them (one of the points best illustrated by Adam Smith). In all these cases inequality of remuneration is necessary to produce equality of attractiveness, and they provide examples of the equalising effect of free competition.

(ii) *Natural monopolies,* such as arise from the greater trust which can be reposed in certain workmen, *e.g.*, goldsmiths and jewellers, or a greater skill, *e.g.*, doctors and lawyers. In these cases the superiority of reward is not a compensation for disadvantages in the employment, but an extra advantage. There was a similar advantage until lately for all who had had even the smallest amount of education, but since reading and writing have been brought into the reach of the multitude, the monopoly price of the lower grade of educated employments has greatly fallen. It must also be remembered that hitherto each employment has been chiefly recruited from the children of those already employed in it, or in similar positions, *e.g.*, the liberal professions by the sons of either the professional or the idle rich; the highly skilled manual employments from the sons of skilled artisans or tradesmen. Consequently the wages of each class have hitherto been regulated by the increase of its own population rather than of the general population of the country. Increased facilities of education, without any check to population, will probably tend to lower the wages of those just above the grade of labourers.

(iii) *Subsidised competition* tends to keep down wages in certain employments, *e.g.*, the numerous opportunities for free education for the Church crowd that profession and produce the wretched wages of curates.

(iv) A similar effect is produced by the competition of *persons with independent means* of support. This cause acts with, if it does not now take the place of, (iii) in the case of men of letters. There are other inducements than money to enter this career, and consequently it is often followed by persons who do not need its pecuniary fruits at all. This also applies sometimes to the clerical profession, and provides the reason why those trades are generally the worst paid in which the wife and children of the artisan aid in the work. The income which the habits of the class demand, and down to which they are almost sure to multiply, is made up in those trades by the earnings of the whole family, while in others the same income must be obtained by the labour of the man alone.

N.B.—This reckoning of wages in families is one of the chief reasons why *the wages of women* are generally lower than those of men. The average wage for a man is reckoned on the basis of his having to support a family: that of a woman on the supposition that she will only have to support herself. No doubt the wages are also affected by custom and the present constitution of Society, which enables men to take systematically the lion's share of whatever belongs to both, and also to the peculiar employments of women, which are usually overstocked, though it is social custom rather than this that accounts for the wages of a manservant being higher than those of a maidservant.

(v) *Restrictive laws*, which limit competition, *e.g.*, apprentice laws, may also affect wages.

(vi) *Custom* rather than competition fixes some wages, *e.g.*, the charges of professional persons, doctors and lawyers.

26. Three-fold Division of the Produce. (II.) Profits.

A. *Analysis of Profits.* The gross profits from Capital are resolvable into three parts:—

(i) *Interest.* This is what is actually paid for the use of the Capital itself, and is as much as a solvent person would be willing to pay for it (*infra*, § 44).

(ii) *Insurance*, or compensation for risk.
[Sometimes called "False interest."]

(iii) *The Wages of Superintendence*, *i.e.*, the remuneration for the devotion of his time and labour by the undertaker of any business. This person may not be the owner of the Capital, and may not get (i) and (ii) or either, but he must get something for his trouble. There are indeed many different ways in which the three parts of profits may be distributed. One man may employ his own Capital and get all three parts, another may take the risk with borrowed Capital and get (ii) and (iii). A sleeping partner may supply part or all of the Capital and receive not merely interest but also a further sum out of the gross profits in compensation for his risk: while sometimes a man may supply the Capital and take the risk and put in a hired servant to manage the business. In any case three things need remuneration—abstinence, risk, exertion.

[N.B.—Only (iii) is now usually treated as profits, and Mill's description of it as the wages of superintendence is not commonly adopted.]

B. *What regulates Profits.*

(i) The *minimum of profits* must be such as, after covering all losses and remunerating the owner for forbearing to consume, provides also a recompense for labour and trouble sufficient to induce persons to undergo it. This minimum is very variable owing to the variations in the first two elements in profits, for the effective desire of accumulation (*supra*, § 15 B) may cause great variations in the rate of interest in different places, while insecurity, *e.g.*, from the rapacity of Governments, may necessitate a high rate of insurance against risk.

(ii) Profits differ *in different employments* to a greater extent than wages, but owing to much the same reason, *e.g.*, profits of retail trade exceed those of wholesale trade because the former has less consideration attached to it than the latter. In this respect the third element in profits is the one chiefly to vary, owing to the more or less skill required by the undertaker, *e.g.*, the high rate of chemists' profits. Natural monopolies also increase profits considerably, *cf.*, gas and water companies.

(iii) Yet the *rate of profit* on Capital in all employments *tends to an equality*. It is clear that the rate of interest does not vary according to the destination of the principal, and though it does vary from time to time according to the circumstances of the market, yet the market rate is at all times a known and definite thing. Yet gross profits would seem to depend on the capacity of individuals, and by their tendency to an equality must therefore be understood not actual equal profits but equal expectations of profits, allowing for any inferiority of the agreeableness or safety of an employment, for if this were not the case, all Capital would be gradually withdrawn from such businesses as give inferior returns and put into the more favourable businesses, and it is indeed this withdrawing from failing businesses and putting of

Capital into thriving ones that prevents the expectations of profit in different employments from continuing very different. This equalising process is not necessarily a very slow one. It is facilitated by credit and by the new accumulations of Capital that take place every year, though it is a slower process if some considerable business has to be abandoned altogether, especially if before one inequality has been corrected, another cause of inequality arises. In general, although profits are very different to different individuals and to the same individual in different years, there cannot be large diversity at the same time and place in the average profits of different employments, except for short periods or when some great permanent revulsion has overtaken a particular trade. It must be noted, however, that competition is not always the determining factor in profits. Custom also has some share in determining it, *e.g.*, the old theory in England that 50% on wholesale prices was the proper rate of profit in retail transactions. If such a custom were to prevail, competition would still operate, but not to the advantage of the consumer. It would only diminish the advantages of the retailers by a greater subdivision of the business.

(iv) *The amount of profits does not depend upon prices.* The money a producer obtains for his commodity is not the cause of his having a profit, but only the mode in which the profit is paid to him. What causes profit is that labour produces more than is required for its support. Now the capitalist advances the wages of labour and (leaving out of consideration the question of rent) he gets back those wages with an additional amount which he takes as profit; therefore

(v) The amount of profits depends on *the magnitude of the produce and the proportion of it obtained by the labourers themselves*, and so profits (according to Ricardo) rise as wages fall and fall as wages rise. Strictly speaking, we should say that profits depend on the cost of labour, *i.e.*, not on what labour brings in to the labourer, but on what it costs the capitalist; for labour, though cheap, may be inefficient, and the varying costliness of what labourers consume affects the relations between wages and the cost of labour, which may thus be regarded as a *function of three variables*, viz., the efficiency of labour, the wages or real reward of the labourer, and the greater or less cost at which the articles composing that reward can be procured, and these circumstances alone can affect profits. Profits would *rise* if labour became more efficient, if its remuneration failed or if the articles the labourers consume became less costly, and profits would *fall* in the contrary cases.

27. Three-fold Division of the Produce. (III.) Rent.

A. *Nature of Rent*. Rent is the effect of a monopoly, and if one man held all the land of a country he could make the rent what he pleased. Such a condition exists where the State owns the land and rent is confounded with taxation. Monopoly exists, however (since land is limited in quantity), even though its owners do not act in concert. Yet a thing thus provided by nature without labour would only command a price if it existed in less quantity than the demand. Now it is seldom that all the land of a country is cultivated. There is, therefore, always some land which does not pay rent, and no land ever pays rent unless in point of fertility and situation it belongs to those superior kinds which exist in less quantity than the demand. Now the worst land which can be cultivated as a means of subsistence is that which will just replace the seed and the food of the labourers employed on it, as such land does not even supply profit, it certainly cannot afford a rent. This is land which must be cultivated by the labourers themselves, and cannot be cultivated as an investment for Capital. Land, which in addition to replacing seed and providing the food of labourers can also pay the ordinary profit on Capital, provides a standard for estimating the amount of rent which will be yielded by all other land, and the theory of rent (associated with the name of Ricardo) is that *the rent which any land will yield is the excess of its produce beyond what would be returned to the same Capital if employed on the worst land in cultivation.* This is not the limit of customary rents, such as Metayer's, but it is the limit of farmers' rents.

B. *Objections to and Modification of the Theory of Rent.*

(i) It is said that *there is no land in cultivation which pays no rent*, but the land that pays no rent does not lie in great masses separate from other land: it is usually mixed up with it, and the person who rents better land obtains inferior soils with it, while his rent for the whole farm is calculated on the produce of those parts alone which are capable of returning more than the common rate of profit. Furthermore, suppose Society wanted a greater increase of produce. If more land could not be put into cultivation, more labour and Capital would have to be applied to the land already cultivated, but unless this were at a time of agricultural invention it would mean a diminished return, and there would always be a point at which it was only just worth while to put more Capital into the land, and therefore, even if it were a fact that there is never any *land* cultivated for which rent is not paid, it would be true that there is always some *agricultural Capital* which pays no rent.

(ii) *The law of rent does not apply in all cases*, for the truths of Political Economy are truths only in the rough. Thus a farmer may pay more than the economic rent for a farm rather than leave one which he has worked for years, *i.e.*, a motive comes into operation which counteracts the economic law, a law that has to proceed on the assumption that men are only guided by economic advantage.

(iii) The value of land may be increased by Capital expended on it. *Is the additional payment that is required for the use of this improved land rent or profit?* It is certainly profit when the improvement is of the nature of buildings which can be distinguished from the land itself. Buildings, like cattle, are not land but Capital regularly consumed and reproduced, but it is possible to conceive improvements, like the draining of the Bedford Level, which are so much part of the land that they cannot be separated from it. The payment for the use of such land has certainly the nature of rent.

(iv) Carey holds that *all rent is the effect of Capital* expended, and that the pecuniary value of all the land in any country is not equal to the amount of Capital that has been expended on it. This implies that the inhabitants, *e.g.*, of England, would not find it worth while to reclaim any new territory that might be added to the country. Such a deduction is contradicted by the facts of the case. Carey makes the mistake of assuming that Capital expended on roads, railways, etc., has the effect of adding value to land generally. As a matter of fact it lowers its value by rendering other and rival lands accessible.

(v) It is said that it is absurd to say that the *cultivation* of inferior land is the cause of rent in the superior. But Ricardo does not say this, he says that the *necessity of cultivating* the inferior land, from the insufficiency of the superior land to feed a growing population, is the cause of rent in the latter.

C. *Relation of Rent to Cost of Production.* Rent (as was assumed *supra*, § 26, B iv) does not enter into the cost of production. Whoever cultivates land, paying a rent for it, gets in return for his rent an instrument of superior power to other instruments of the same kind for which no rent is paid The superiority is in exact proportion to the rent. So the real expenses of production are those incurred on the worst land, and rent need not therefore be calculated among them.

28. Value.

I. *Preliminary Remarks and Definitions.* The Exchange of commodities (which the division of labour renders more and more imperative) gives rise to the problem of Value. This has appeared to some writers to be a subject coextensive with Political Economy itself, and they have proposed to re-name the science either Catallactics (the Science of Exchanges), or the Science of Values, but Value affects the production of Wealth not at all, and its distribution only so far as competition is the distributing agency, and to regard this as the all-important side of the subject is to make the error of not distinguishing between necessities arising from the nature of things and those created by social arrangements.

In discussing Value it is necessary to distinguish at the outset—

(i) *Value in Use.* Here the word "Use" is not employed as opposed to pleasure, but as a capacity to satisfy a desire or serve a purpose. Adam Smith is confusing the two uses of the word when he says that "Diamonds have a great value in exchange but little value in use." As a matter of fact diamonds satisfy a very potent desire and therefore have a great value in use, which thus implies the utmost value which persons will put upon a thing as a means of gratifying their inclinations.

[The term "Utility" is now usually employed for Value in Use.]

(ii) *Exchange Value,* which means the general power of purchasing possessed by a thing. This may fall short of (i), but it can never exceed it, because people obviously will not give for a thing more than the utmost value which they themselves put on it.

[The word "Value" used by itself always means "Exchange Value."]

(iii) *Price, i.e.,* the value of a thing in relation to money, while, as we have seen, Value means command over commodities in general.

II. *Relations between Value and Price.*

(i) Price often acts as a guide to a rise or fall in the value of an article. It has been said that Value means command over commodities in general. Now a coat, *e.g.*, may command a great deal of bread and very few precious stones, and it may command more or less of either of these other commodities at different times, but we cannot tell from these variations whether the coat itself has risen or fallen in value unless we happen to know of some circumstances which has directly affected the coat itself; but we may be able to tell whether there has been a change in the value of the coat if its price has changed (unless something has affected the value of money).

(ii) On the other hand it must be remembered that Value is a relative term, and that therefore *there cannot be a general rise or fall of Values.* If prices generally go up or down it must mean that there has been a change in the value of money. Thus a general rise or fall in Prices only affects those persons who are the holders of money or who, like annuitants or debtors, expect to receive or to pay money.

III. *Competition and the Laws of Value.* Values can be reduced to any assignable law only in so far as they are determined by competition. Therefore the laws of Value will only apply to mercantile Values and Prices, where the axiom is true that *there cannot be for the same article of the same quality two prices in the same market.* The laws will have to be qualified in order to meet the case of retail prices which from various causes, chiefly the habits of customers (people think it fine to pay and ask no questions), are not so directly affected by competition, and therefore in all reasoning on this point the proviso must be understood, " supposing all parties to take care of their own interest."

IV. There are two conditions of Value—

(i) *Utility.* No one will pay for anything which he does not want.

(ii) *Difficulty of Attainment.* No one will pay for anything that he can obtain gratuitously and without effort. Now there are various kinds of (ii), according to which commodities may be grouped in the following classes:—

A. Things of which it is physically impossible to increase the quantity beyond certain limits, *e.g.*, old pictures, rare books, special sights in towns, etc.

B. The majority of things bought and sold belong to a class in which the obstacle to attainment consists only in the labour and expense requisite to produce the commodity.

C. Commodities which can be multiplied to an indefinite extent by labour and expenditure, but not by a fixed amount of labour and expenditure, *e.g.*, agricultural produce.

The Laws of Value affecting A, B and C may be treated separately.

29. A. Commodities limited in Quantity.

I. *The Problem Stated.* When things are absolutely limited in quantity some say that their value depends upon their scarcity, but this expression is not sufficiently definite; others say that it depends on (i) the Demand; (ii) the Supply. This needs explanation—

(i) Demand does *not* = desire. A beggar may desire a diamond, but his desire would have no influence on its price. Demand = the wish to possess combined with the power of purchasing (sometimes called " Effectual Demand.")

(ii) Supply = the quantity offered for sale. It has been said that value depends upon the ratio between (i) and (ii), but the phrase is not sufficiently precise. What ratio can there be between a quantity and a desire even when combined with a demand. There can only be a ratio between the quantity demanded and the quantity supplied, but the quantity demanded varies according to the value, and the demand therefore partly depends on the value which was supposed to depend on it. What is the solution of this paradox?

II. *The Relation of Demand and Supply.* Suppose that the demand for a thing exceeds its supply, *i.e.*, there are persons ready to buy at the market value a greater quantity than is offered for sale. Competition takes place on the side of the buyers, the value rises, but not necessarily in the ratio of the deficiency, because the demand, *e.g.*, of on article of necessity, may still exceed the supply even when the Value is raised far above the original deficiency, and equally the demand may fall below the supply if a rise short of the deficiency has put the article beyond the purses or inclinations of would-be purchasers. At what point then will the rise be arrested? At the point wherever it be which equalises the demand and the supply, either by keeping off from the demand or by bringing forward additional sellers to supply it.

Next, suppose the supply to exceed the demand. Competition will now be on the side of the sellers. The demand can only be made up a cheapening of the article to bring it within the reach of more numerous customers. The amount of the fall in value required differs in different cases. It is usually greatest in the case of absolute necessaries or the luxuries of a small class. In the case of food those who have enough do not require more on account of cheapness, and therefore when there is an abundant harvest there is usually a withdrawal of part of the supply, but where the article is cheapened or withdrawn, the result is an equalization of Demand and Supply.

The law therefore of the value of the commodities under discussion can be expressed by *the equation of Demand and Supply*, *i.e.*, if the demand increases the value rises; if the demand diminishes the value falls; if the supply falls off the value rises; if the supply is increased the value falls, and the rise or the fall continues until the demand and supply are again equal to one another.

III. *Miscellaneous Cases falling under this Law.*

(i) *Monopolised Commodities.* The price of these does not depend solely on the will of the monopolist. He cannot fix it at more than the buyer's extreme estimate of its worth to himself, and he cannot fix it at that unless he limits the supply. De Quincey gives an example of a huckster in the wilds of America selling a musical box worth six guineas for sixty guineas. He could not have obtained that extreme price for both if he had offered two musical boxes for sale. Monopoly Value therefore does not depend on any peculiar principle, but is a mere variety of the ordinary case of demand and supply.

(ii) Some commodities are *temporarily insusceptible of increase*, *e.g.*, agricultural produce. Till the next harvest corn is practically assimilated to things of which the quantity cannot be increased. If the demand for such commodities increases the value will temporarily rise so as to accommodate the demand to the supply.

(iii) There are some articles whose supply may be definitely increased but *cannot be rapidly diminished*, *e.g.*, gold and houses. The value of these things may continue for a long time so low as to put a complete stop to further production. Till the supply is diminished by a wearing-out process, the value will be regulated solely by the supply and demand.

(iv) There are commodities indefinitely capable of increase, or decrease, whose value never depends upon anything but demand and supply. This is the case with the commodity Labour.

30. B. Commodities reproducible without Increase of Cost.

I. *Law of their Value: Cost of Production.* Nothing will be sold for any length of time at less than is sufficient to repay its cost of production, and no Capitalist will go on permanently producing things at a profit less than he can live on. Thus the cost of production with the ordinary profit is the necessary price of all things made by Labour and Capital, and with regard to commodities which are susceptible of indefinite multiplication without increase of cost, this necessary value is not only the minimum with which the producers will be content, but also, if competition is free, the maximum which they can expect. If any more than this value is achieved by such commodities, Capital will speedily be attracted to the making of them, and the value will fall. Thus, as a general rule, things tend to exchange for one another at such values as will enable each producer to be repaid the cost of production with the ordinary profit. So the value of a thing which is proportional to its cost of production has been called its Natural Value or Price. It is the point about which value oscillates and to which it always tends to return.

II. *What tends to keep them at this Value.* The latent influence by which the values of things are made to conform in the long run to the cost of production is the variation that would otherwise take place in the supply of the commodity. That supply would be increased if a thing rose above its natural value and diminished if it fell below it, and these alterations of supply need not be actual—they may be potential. The mere possibility of an increase or diminution of supply will cause dealers who are aware of what will happen to alter their prices. It does not, as a matter of fact, always happen that the cheaper production of an article followed by a lowering of its price will cause an increase of supply; it will depend upon whether a greater quantity is wanted at the reduced value. Certain things, *e.g.*, silk handkerchiefs, will sell in greater quantities if they are cheaper, but a man does not buy more steam engines or wine vaults because their price is lowered; on the other hand if the value of a thing rose through some increase in the cost of production, the supply would only be diminished if the demand were, and there are many articles for which it requires a very considerable rise of price materially to reduce the demand, *e.g.*, bread. Thus the value of these commodities depends on the cost of production and not upon demand and supply, which indeed depends also upon the cost of production, for the demand for a certain thing at its cost value will produce a supply to conform to it, and the equation of demand and supply operates to restore the natural value when, for any reason, the market value deviates from it.

III. *Analysis of Cost of Production.*

(i) The principal element in the cost of production is the quantity of Labour, and in estimating this quantity it is necessary to take into consideration both the Labour directly employed about the thing produced and that employed in operations preparatory to its production (*supra*, § 6).

(ii) Wages are only an element in the cost of production in so far as they vary from employment to employment. A rise or fall of general wages is a fact which affects all commodities in the same manner, and therefore affords no reason why they should exchange for each other in one rather than in another proportion. To suppose that high wages make high values is to suppose that there can be such a thing as general high values (*supra*, 28, II., ii). However, if wages are higher in one employment than another, or if they rise or fall permanently in one employment without doing so in others, these inequalities do really operate upon Values, for they evidently alter the *relative* costs of production of different commodities.

(iii) Profits too are an element in the cost of production in so far as they vary from employment to employment, or are spread over unequal lengths of time. Variations occur because there must be compensation for superior risk, trouble and disagreeableness, *e.g.*, gunpowder exchanges for other things in a higher ratio than that of the labour required from first to last in producing it, and again some things, *e.g.*, wine, improve by keeping; others, *e.g.*, cloth do not, but a dealer will not keep wine say for five years if he cannot sell it at the end of that time for as much more than the cloth as amounts to five years' profit accumulated at compound interest.

For a similar reason profits will enter more into the cost of production of things made by machinery than of things made directly by Labour, and the more durable the machinery is the more will profits enter into the cost. From these inequalities arise the following consequences:—

(*a*) That commodities do not exchange in the ratio simply of the quantities of labour required to produce them, and

(*b*) That every rise or fall of general profits will have an effect on values, not indeed by raising or lowering them generally, but by altering the proportion in which the values of things are affected by the unequal lengths of time for which profit is due. For the same reason even *a general rise of wages does in some degree influence values*, because an increase in the cost of labour lowers profits and therefore lowers in natural value the things into which profits enter in a greater proportion than the average, and raises those in which they enter in a less proportion than the average.

(iv) Besides these necessary elements in the cost of production, there are some that occur occasionally, such as taxes which are raised on particular commodities and so cause their value to rise, and Scarcity Value of the materials which may be necessary for the manufacture of certain commodities, but this Scarcity Value chiefly operates in the case of natural agents, *i.e.*, that element in production which pays rent. This chiefly affects the third class, whose Law of Value needs to be investigated.

31. **C. Commodities reproducible with Increase of Cost.**

(i) *Law of their Value.* The principal one of the commodities which can always be increased in quantity by Labour and Capital, but not by the same amount of Labour and Capital is agricultural produce, *i.e.*, the things in which land plays a direct part as a productive agent, and which are therefore subject to the Law of Diminishing Return (*supra,* § 15 C.).

Supposing that a new demand for wheat occurs when the price is 20/- a quarter, and that this demand cannot be met except by cultivating inferior land or expending more Capital and Labour over the existing land so that the existing amount of wheat can only be produced at a cost which 25/- per quarter will remunerate; it will clearly be necessary to pay 25/- a quarter for wheat under the new conditions; for we are not able to buy one loaf cheaper than another, because the corn from which it is made being grown on a richer soil has cost less to the grower : so the Law of Value of these commodities is *the cost of production in the most unfavourable existing circumstances.*

(ii) *Rent in Relation to Value.* This brings us by another road to the Law of Rent (*supra,* § 27). Rent is the difference between the unequal returns to different parts of the Capital employed on the soil. It is not true to say that the produce of land is always at a Monopoly Value because it yields rent in addition to the ordinary rate of profit; a thing cannot be at a Monopoly Value when its supply can be increased to an indefinite extent if you are only willing to incur the cost. *Rent therefore forms no part of the cost of production* which determines the value of agricultural produce, though it might do so if we can suppose the population increasing to such an extent while cut off from external supplies that both the land and its produce would really rise to a monopoly price : as it is, rent merely equalises the profits of different farming capitals by enabling the landlord to appropriate all extra gains occasioned by superiority of natural advantages, and is therefore, unless artificially increased by restrictive laws, no burden on the consumer.

(iii) *Rent of Mines, Fisheries, etc.* Mines and fisheries and lakes and rivers (not in the open sea) are subject to the Law of Rent because those of different degrees of productivity are being used at the same time, but as these are comparatively few, their qualities do not graduate gently into one another as the qualities of land do, and it is possible that the demand for their produce may so rise as to bring it to a *Scarcity Value*. The opening of a new mine or fishery will lower value by an increase of the supply. This may result in an inferior mine or fishery being abandoned, and if the superior ones, with the addition of the new one, produce as much of the commodity as is required at the lower value, the fall of value will be permanent, and there will be a corresponding fall in the rents of those mines or fisheries which are not abandoned.

As to the case of a ground rent of buildings, this will not be less than the rent which the same land would afford in agriculture, but may be greater to an indefinite amount, either in consideration of beauty or of convenience. Sites of remarkable beauty may be at a Scarcity Value; sites superior only in convenience are governed as to their value by the ordinary principles of Rent.

(iv) Cases of extra profit analogous to rent, *e.g.*, a patent or exclusive privilege for the use of a process by which cost of production is lessened. If the value of the product continues to be regulated by what it costs to those who are obliged to persist in the old process, the patentee will make an extra profit equal to his advantage. *This extra profit is similar to rent:* so are the extra gains which any producer obtains through superior talents for business or superior business arrangements. All advantages, in fact, which one competitor has over another, whether natural or acquired, bring his commodity into this class and assimilate the possessor of the advantage to a receiver of rent. [Cp. Walker's Theory of Profits.]

32. Modification of Theory of Value.

The theory of Value expressed in the above four

sections contemplates a system of production carried on by capitalists for profit, and is modified—

(i) By the case of *labourers cultivating for subsistence;* for a peasant who supports himself and his family with one portion of his produce will often sell the remainder for very much what would be its cost value to the capitalist; but even here there is a minimum of value. He must sell at a sufficient amount to purchase his necessaries and to pay his rent, which may be in his case determined by custom, or by the competition of persons to obtain land, and does not therefore follow the ordinary Law of Rent, but *is in this case an element of the cost of production.* Yet it cannot be said that the value of what he sells depends at all on the cost of production. It depends entirely on demand and supply, *i.e.*, on the proportion between the quantity of surplus food which the peasants choose to produce and the numbers of the non-peasant population.

(ii) By the case of *slave labour.* The slave owner is a Capitalist and his profit must amount to the ordinary rate. In respect to expenses he is in the same position as if his slaves were free labourers hired at wages equal to the present cost. If the cost is less than the wages of free labour would be, his profits are greater, but the values of commodities would not be affected unless the privilege of cheap labour is confined to particular branches of production, and this would affect prices and values just as all cases of inequality between the wages of different employments. Slave-grown will exchange for non-slave-grown commodities in a less ratio than that of the quantity of labour required for their production.

33. Money.

A. The *functions* of a Circulating Medium are:—

(i) To provide a *common measure* of values. This could be done by imaginary units of calculation, as certain African tribes compare the values of articles in macutes which are not real things.

(ii) To avoid the inconveniences of barter by providing a commodious *means of exchange.* This is by far the most important use of money. Consider the difficulties of a hungry tailor with a coat to dispose of by barter—(*a*) the discovery of a man with bread who wanted a coat, and (*b*) the necessity of buying more bread than he wanted at one time.

[(iii) To provide a *standard* for future payments (see *infra*, B. vi)].

B. *Gold* and *Silver* are best fitted for the purposes of money, because they are—

(i) *Desirable,* next to food and clothing, personal ornament is the strongest inclination in rude society.

(ii) *Imperishable,* unlike food and clothing.

(iii) *Portable.*

(v) *Divisible,* unlike jewels.

(vi) *Of comparatively fixed value.* This is a quality whose importance has only been recognised since the other qualities originally recommended the pretty general adoption of the precious metals. Fluctuations have occurred in the value of gold and silver, chiefly owing to the discovery of mines, but on the whole no commodities are so little exposed to causes of variation. Therefore gold and silver are more fit than any other commodity to be *the subject of engagements for receiving or paying a given quantity at some distant period.*

N.B.—Coining, which avoids the necessity of weighing and assaying on every occasion, has been a natural development from the adoption of the precious metals for money. Governments have usually taken this operation into their own hands and their guarantee is usually the most reliable, but they have not hesitated at times to lower the standard of the coinage in their own interests—which is barefaced robbery.

C. The *Value* of Money (a phrase which is sometimes used for, but must be distinguished from, the Value of Capital, or Interest). Money, being a mere contrivance for facilitating exchanges, does not interfere with the operations of the laws of Value. The only new relation between commodities that is introduced is their relation to the commodity, money. The value of money is therefore determined like that of other commodities, *i.e.*,

(1) Its temporary value depends on demand and supply.
(2) Its average or permanent value on the cost of production.

But these laws need special elucidation in their application to money.

1. The *supply of money* consists of all the money in circulation at the time, and the *demand for money* consists of all the goods offered for sale. The money and the goods are reciprocally supply and demand to one another. If all the money in the possession of each person in a country were doubled the price of every other commodity would be doubled, or, in other words, the value of money would be halved. That is to say that, supposing the wants and inclinations of a community remain the same so that the relative values of other commodities do not change, *the value of money is in exact proportion to its quantity*, and unlike the value of other things which are desired for themselves. But this does not mean that the amount of money in circulation is equal in value to the whole of the goods in a country. Money passes from hand to hand and must be counted as often as it is used, and similarly goods must generally be counted more than once before they are finally bought for consumption. Therefore in estimating the value of money it is necessary also to take into consideration *the rapidity of its circulation*, a phrase which suggests how often money changes hands in a given time, but which must here be taken to mean how often it changes hands to perform a given amount of transactions. (Perhaps "efficiency of money" is a

better expression). Thus the value of money depends temporarily on its *quantity* and the *rapidity of circulation*. But this principle is liable in practice to many limitations—

(i) The influence of credit (*infra*, § 35 B).

(ii) Money hoarded does not affect prices.

(iii) Money invested as Capital may only affect the market of securities.

(iv) Periodic increases of the money in circulation, as when dividends are paid at the Bank, do not affect prices.

2. The value of money, permanently, and in a state of freedom (*i.e.*, where the Government does not charge a seignorage for coining and so enhance the value of the coined metal), conforms to the *value of bullion contained in it*, which is determined by the *cost of production* and, as the precious metals are the produce of mines, this cost is the cost in labour and expense at the worst mine which it is necessary to work to obtain the required supply (*supra*, § 31). The producer of gold will increase or diminish his production according to the amount of his profits, and in this way the value of gold is made to conform to the cost of production of the metal, but an adjustment takes long to effect in a commodity so generally desired and so durable.

Though the value of Money depends on the Cost of Production, the principle expressed in 1 must not be discarded for—

(i) It is simply the law of supply and demand, and the cost of production would have no effect on value if it had none on supply.

(ii) There is a closer connexion between the value and quantity of money than between the value and quantity of other things, for a potential alteration in supply affects other commodities while it requires an actual one to affect the precious metals when they are used as money.

Yet every country will tend to have in circulation just that quantity of money which will perform all the exchanges required of it, consistently with maintaining a value conformable to its cost of production.

N.B.—The law of the Cost of Production only applies to the places in which the precious metals are produced. Money, as an imported commodity, depends for its value on the cost of production of what is given in exchange for it (*infra* § 41).

34. Bimetallism or Token Money?

It is an obvious convenience to use the two precious metals for the circulating medium, the more costly for larger payments and the cheaper one for smaller. The question is, how can this best be done?

A. It may be done by establishing a fixed proportion between the two metals, *e.g.*, one gold coin to twenty silver ones and allowing everyone to pay in either metal, and thus establishing a *Double Standard* [or what is now termed *Bimetallism*, which was not a prominent subject of controversy when Mill wrote]. The proportion, when first made, would correspond to the relative values of the two metals grounded on their cost of production. But the values of the gold or the silver might vary, *e.g.*, silver was lowered in value permanently by the discovery of the American mines. Then all debtors would pay in coins of relatively less valuable metal, and the coins of the other could be melted down, as the bullion would be more valuable than the money. Then the standard would really be not that of both metals together but that of the one most suited to debtors at the particular time, and the value of money would be liable to the variations in value of two metals, instead of only one where one alone is made legal tender. [It is held by Bimetallists that the action of Demand and Supply would tend to bring back the two metals to the relative values of the ratio paid for the currency.]

B. Another plan is to have one metal, usually

the more costly, as the standard [mono-metallism] but to use the other for *subsidiary coins* [token money] and make them legal tender for small amounts. Such subsidiary coins must be rated somewhat above their intrinsic value, so that an increase in the value of metal should not make it worth while to melt down the coins, and they must be limited in quantity, so that there should be no inducement to buy the metal and send it to be coined. On the other hand too high a valuation should not be put on such coins or there will be a strong temptation to private coining.

35. Credit.

A. *The function of Credit in Production.* The extension of credit is not equivalent to the creation of Capital. If A borrows Capital from B the use of it rests with A alone, even though B may reckon it as still part of his wealth and even obtain on the strength of it the use of another Capital from C. But credit does assist production :—

(i) By transferring Capital to those who can use it most efficiently. Funds that would lie idle, especially many small sums in the hands of bankers, become employed productively and not merely by being transferred from those who will not use them to those who will, but also by turning the undeveloped talent of the country to better account by enabling persons with business talent but without Capital to use their capacities to the increase of the public wealth.

N.B.—These considerations only apply to credit given to the industrial classes; credit given by buyers to unproductive consumers has an opposite effect. It hands over, not the Capital of the unproductive classes to the productive, but that of the productive to the unproductive.

(ii) By economising the use of money, which credit effects by various methods and instruments.

(*a*) *Book Credit.* A and B have dealings with one another and give one another credit till the end of the year, when the money that changes hands is only the balance of all their transactions. In this way a single payment of £100 may liquidate a long series of transactions amounting to several thousands.

(*b*) *Bills of Exchange.* A may pay his debts to B by making over to him a debt due to himself from C. This is conveniently done by a transferable order by A on C, which when authenticated by C's signature becomes an acknowledgement of debt.

The uses of such bills, in the order of their development, are:—

(i) To save the expense and risk of transferring the precious metals from place to place. By this means debtors *e.g.* in York may pay creditors in London by transferring to them debts due to them from other persons in London.

(ii) To enable the trader who gives long credit to raise money before it is due to him from the debtor. This he can do by discounting his debtors' Bills with a money lender: *i.e.* transferring the Bill to him and receiving the amount minus Interest for the time it has still to run.

(iii) To raise money by *Accommodation* or *Fictitious* Bills which are not grounded on any debt previously due. Such Bills agree with real Bills in being discountable articles and in increasing the circulating medium and, if not in representing actual property, at any rate in representing it as much as a second or third real Bill drawn by a second or third dealer in the same goods. Such Bills differ from real Bills in so far as they profess to be what they are not, in that they are less likely to be punctually paid and in that they are less subject to limitation as to quantity.

When discounted a Bill of Exchange no longer performs the functions of money but is itself bought and sold for money, but if is paid by one person to another in discharge of a debt it does something for which, if the Bill did not exist, money would be required, and many Bills are at last presented for payment quite covered with endorsements, each of which represents a transaction in which the Bill has performed the function of money.

(*c*) *Promissory Notes* A Bill drawn upon anyone and accepted by him and a Note of Hand by him promising to pay the same sum are, as far as he is concerned, exactly equivalent, except that the former generally bears Interest and the latter does not; and that the former is commonly payable after a certain lapse of time and the latter at sight. This is a convenient way of employing credit in lending money, but as such Notes are payable on demand, the issuer will usually have to keep by him as much money as will enable him to pay any such claims as can be expected to occur. Governments have not been slow to use this expedient, because it is the only mode in which they can borrow money without paying Interest; their promises to pay being, in the estimation of the holders, equivalent to money in hand.

(*d*) *Cheques.* The custom of keeping deposits at banks and making payments by cheques enables a great many transactions to take place without any money changing hands. It is clear that if the person making a payment by cheque and the person receiving it keep their money with the same banker the payment takes place by a mere transfer in the bankers' books. And the establishment of the Clearing House in London, where all cheques drawn on London and many country banks are balanced against one another, enables transactions representing millons of pounds of money to be carried out with the actual transference of a few thousand pounds.

13. *Influence of Credit on Prices.*

(i) Credit and not its Instruments affect Prices.

Credit does not affect permanent value in money, but immediate and temporary prices may deviate widely from the standard of cost of production, according to the quantity of money in circulation. Now Bills of Exchange, Cheques, etc., circulate as money, and perform the functions of it. Does an increase of the quantity of transferable paper tend to raise prices in the same manner as an increase of the quantity of money, or is it not true to say that what does act on prices is credit, in whatever shape given, and whether giving rise to any transferable instrument or not? Money acts on prices through demand, and though in the long run the money which people lay out will be the same amount as the money which they have to lay out, yet this is not the case at any given time. Sometimes they keep money by them for fear of an emergency, but the converse is the commoner case. People make purchases with money not in their possession. An article paid for by cheque is paid with money which is not only not in the payer's possession, but generally not even in the banker's. Thus the amount of purchasing power which a person can exercise is composed of all the money in his possession, or due to him, and of all his credit. And it is credit itself, not the form or mode in which it is given, which may be the operating cause in creating a demand which will help to raise prices.

(ii) It is the influence of credit in causing a rise of prices that produces *commercial crises.* If the price of a particular article is caused to rise by money demand alone an unusual proportion of money would be drawn from other commodities and other prices would fall. But in times of speculation credit as well as money is strained to the utmost to cause a demand for all commodities in which a rise is expected, and in which, in consequence of the demand, a rise takes place. After a time those who buy wish to sell and prices collapse. Then occurs a commercial crisis, when a great number of merchants and traders at once have a difficulty in meeting their engagements. The crisis that followed the speculative year 1825 was of such a nature. And in such crises there is a contraction of credit corresponding to the extension which produces it. (The circumstances which caused the crises of 1847 and 1865 were not, however, of this kind, but due to great foreign payments and the large conversion of circulating Capital into fixed Capital, which affected the Loan Market).

(iii) The form which credit takes only affects prices in so far as it gives greater facility for credit transactions. Thus Bills are a more powerful instrument for acting on prices than book credits, and bank notes than Bills. But the distinction is of little practical importance because the multiplication of bank notes and other transferable paper does not for the most part accompany and facilitate speculation, but comes into play chiefly when the tide is turning and difficulties begin to be felt, while book credits are not great instruments of speculative purchases. Cheques again are an instrument for acting on prices equally powerful with bank notes.

(iv) Are these forms of credit to be regarded as money? This is merely a question of nomenclature, since money and credit are exactly on a par in their effect on prices. An inconvertible paper which is Legal Tender is certainly money, but are Bank of England notes, which are convertible? An instrument which would be deprived of all value by the insolvency of a corporation cannot be money in any sense in which money is opposed to credit. It may be most suitably described as *coined credit*. The other forms of credit may be distinguished from it as *credit in ingots.* There is therefore no generic distinction between bank notes and other forms of credit.

36. Inconvertible Paper Money.

A. Since the value of inconvertible paper money depends wholly on its quantity it is a *matter of arbitrary regulation.* The result of any issue of such money will be to raise prices to the extent to which such issue increases the existing currency. The result will be that metal money will be melted down to take advantage of the increased prices until sufficient metal money has been removed from circulation to restore the total amount of the currency to the old figure. Further issues of paper would have the same series of effects until the paper currency has been entirely substituted for the metal one. (In a country without metal mines and with foreign trade the metal money will leave the country sooner than be melted down.) It is at this point, where the currency of the country has become a wholly paper one, that the different effects of convertible and inconvertible paper will begin to be felt. For the issue of convertible paper will have to cease when there is no more specie to meet it; but to the increase of inconvertible currency there is no check and the issuers may depreciate the currency without limit.

B. An inconvertible paper currency *regulated by the price of bullion* might be safe, but it would have little to recommend it over convertible paper, to which it would conform exactly in its variations save exemption from the necessity of keeping a reserve, and, as a Government need never keep a large reserve, this is unimportant. It would, moreover, lead to fraudulent tampering with the price of bullion for the sake of acting on the currency; and there would always be the temptation to over-issue.

C. Advocates of an inconvertible paper currency hold (i) that it is quite safe if it represents actual property; (ii) that in increasing the currency it promotes industry.

(i) *Refutation.* What is the good of paper representing property which cannot be claimed in exchange for the notes? It may be said that it is a guarantee of the final solvency of the issue. But insolvency is only one of the evils to which a paper currency is liable. Another evil is depreciation in value from excessive issue, cf. the *Assignats* of the French Revolution, which were supposed to represent the lands of the Crown, the Church, etc. They depreciated to such an extent that the result was that at last an assignat of 600 frs. was required to pay for a pound of butter. This, however, represented land in general. Would it be possible to have paper representing a definite quantity of land? The plan would certainly have advantages over that which was pursued, and might be an assistance in selling rapidly a great quantity of land with the least possible sacrifice. But what advantage would a currency convertible into land (which is more variable in value than gold, and is to most persons an encumbrance rather than a desirable possession) have over a currency convertible into coin?

(ii) *Refutation.* The rise in prices certainly stimulates industry, but if there is a general rise in prices brought about by an issue of paper money what will be the gain for those who have speculated in the rise except a *few more tickets to count by*? Even supposing that all commodities did not rise in price simultaneously, only a seller of those commodities which were the first to rise would gain; the seller of those which were slowest to rise would lose, and thus one dealer's industry would be encouraged at the expense of another's. In fine, there is no way in which the depreciation of money can benefit anybody except at the expense of somebody else.

D. Depreciation of currency is a form of *tax on the community*, which acts as a *fraud on creditors*, who lose by having their debts paid them in a currency which is less valuable than when the debts were incurred. Conversely it has been argued that when Peel's Bill in 1819 restored cash payments at the original standard an injustice was done to borrowers who had obtained their loans when the currency was depreciated, but it is doubtful whether the currency was depreciated during the Bank Restriction; and it must also be remembered that many of the obligations were incurred before the Bank Restriction. Also, apart from the facts, there is a question of principle. Even supposing we were now paying Interest on such a debt in a currency 50% more valuable than that in which it was contracted, what difference would this make in the obligation of paying it if the condition that it should be so paid were part of the original compact?

37. Problems of Value connected with Price.

A. Can there be an *over-supply of commodities* generally? Though an over-supply or glut of any one commodity may, acting through the law of supply and demand, cause it to be sold temporarily at a loss, yet there cannot, as some writers have held, be a general over-supply of all commodities (*supra* § 9 A). Now these writers when they speak of supply of commodities outrunning the demand may mean by demand (i) means of purchase, or (ii) the desire to possess.

(i) Supposing there to be the desire to possess, how can there be a deficiency of demand for all commodities for want of the means of payment? For the means of payment for commodities is commodities, and anything which increases the supply of commodities in every market would also increase to the same extent the purchasing power. It is a sheer absurdity that all things should fall in value and that all producers should in consequence be insufficiently remunerated. When the values remain the same, price does not matter, even supposing that the commodity, money, were not increased in quantity to the same extent as other commodities.

(ii) Suppose, then, that the desire to possess falls short, and that the general produce of industry may be greater than is the desire for consumption by that part of the community which has the equivalent to give. Now there may certainly be a greater quantity of one particular commodity than is so desired, and it is abstractly conceivable that this may be the case with all commodities, but as whoever brings additional commodities to the market brings additional power to purchase, so he also brings the additional desire to consume, and, moreover, those who have enough of everything employ their savings in employing labour productively, *i.e.*, they make over the surplus of their purchasing power for the general benefit of the labouring classes by giving them productive employment, and until the working classes also reach the point of satiety there will be no want of demand for the produce of Capital, however rapidly it may accumulate.

In fact the theory of over-supply is an error which has arisen from a wrong interpretation of the phenomena of a commercial crisis. Such a crisis is not the effect of a general excess of production, but the consequence of an excess of speculative purchase. It is not a gradual advent of low prices, but a sudden recoil from prices extraordinarily high. It may also be due to an erroneous interpretation of the fall of profits and interest which takes place with the progress of population and production, and is in reality due to an increase of population and of demand for food, which produce an increased cost of maintaining labour. Low profits are quite a different thing from deficiency of demand.

B. *Measure of Value.*

(i) Can there be a measure of *exchange value ?*

Any commodity will serve as such a measure at a given time and place. When one thing is worth two pounds and another three, one is worth two-thirds of the other. Money is a complete measure of their value. But what some political economists want is a measure of the value of some thing at different times and places. They want some means of ascertaining the value of a commodity by merely comparing it with the measure, without referring it specially to any other given commodity. The great difficulty in the way of this is the necessary indefiniteness of the idea of general exchange value, *i.e.*, value in relation, not to some one commodity, but to commodities at large.

(ii) Can there be a measure of *cost of production* which would serve as a sort of measure of value? Some writers have imagined a commodity as invariably produced by the same quantity of labour. Even if we found that the fixed Capital employed in the production of the commodity always bore the same proportion to the labour on it, such a commodity would still be by no means constant in its extremes of value, because, apart from the temporary fluctuations caused by Supply and Demand, its exchange value would be altered by every change in the circumstances of production of the things against which it was exchanged. But still such a commodity would serve as a measure, not of the value but of the cost of production of other things. But there is no such commodity; everything varies more or less, even gold and silver, in cost of production. Adam Smith suggested two commodities—

(*a*) Corn, whose value, though it fluctuates from year to year, does not vary much from century to century. A view which is erroneous, because corn tends to rise in cost of production with every increase of population and to fall with every improvement in agriculture.

(*b*) Labour, with regard to which his language is not uniform, as he sometimes calls it a good measure only for short periods, saying that the value of labour does not vary much from year to to year, and at other times as if it were the most proper measure of value, because one day's muscular exertion of one man may be looked upon as always to mean the same kind of effort or sacrifice.

This, however, is to impart an idea analogous to Value in Use: one day's labour in one country may produce twice as much as in another. Therefore it is absurd to say that the value in exchange of the labour in each country is the same.

N.B.—Distinguish measure of value from regulator of value. When Adam Smith says that labour is a measure of value he means not the labour by which the thing is made, but the quantity of labour which it will exchange for. When Ricardo says that the value of a thing is regulated by the quantity of labour he means the quantity required for producing it which determines its value. To confound these two ideas would be like confounding the thermometer with the fire.

38. Some peculiar Cases of Value.

I. *Commodities which have a joint cost of production, e.g.,* gas and coke. In such cases the Law of Demand and Supply regulates the amount of the cost of production which goes to create the values of each. Suppose gas to find an easy market at a certain price but that there is not a sufficient demand for all the coke produced with it, coke will have to be reduced in price to an extent that will permit the joint price of the gas and coke paying for the concern; consequently the price of the gas will have to be raised and the demand will contract so that the production will be somewhat reduced; and prices will become stationary when, by the joint effect of the rise of gas and the fall of coke, so much less of the first is sold, and so much more of the second, that there is now a market for all the coke which results from the existing extent of the gas manufacture. A converse process will take place if more coke is wanted than can be supplied with the existing amount of gas. Therefore the natural values relatively to each other of two such commodities are those which will create a demand for each in the ratio of the quantities in which they are produced.

II. Values of *different kinds of Agricultural Produce.* The natural value (*e.g.*, of wheat and oats) is the cost of production of each on the medium soils which are about equally suited for producing both. But the effect of demand may be *e.g.*, that wheat will have to be grown on soil better suited for oats, and then the relative value must be in proportion to the cost of production on that quality of land on which the comparative demand for the two grains requires that both of them should be grown. Here again demand is not an occasional disturber of value, but a permanent regulator of it, supplementary to the cost of production.

39. International Trade.

A. *Nature.* International Trade and Commerce does not arise merely because one country can produce a thing which another cannot, nor even because one country can produce it better than another. England may import corn from Poland and pay for it in cloth, even though England has a decided advantage over Poland in the production of both one and the other. In other words *cost of production is not a regulator of international values.* Capital and Labour do not migrate easily, and in consequence the profits may be so different in different places as to make it worth while to import commodities to a place where they can be produced with equal or greater facility in order to reap the superior advantage of a market for the goods which are sent in exchange for them. The matter is capable of simple illustration. Suppose both cloth and corn require 100 days' labour in Poland and 150 days' labour in England: then cloth of 150 days' labour in England = cloth of 100 days' labour in Poland and would exchange for corn of 100 days' labour which in England would = 150 days' labour. In such a case there would be no advantage in exchanging the commodities, even apart from cost of carriage, etc. But supposing the other figures remained the same, save that the corn cost 200 days' labour in England: then England with her 150 days' labour could procure in Poland what would cost 200 days' labour and effect a saving of 50 days' labour; though to enable Poland to gain anything by the exchange something must be abated from the gain of England. The corn produced in Poland by a 100 days' labour must be paid for by England by more cloth than Poland could produce by that kind of labour. Thus the exchange of commodities between distant places is determined by differences, not in their absolute, but in their comparative cost of production.

B. The benefits of commerce are

(i) Direct. *An increased efficiency of the productive powers of the world*, *i.e.*, the direct advantage of foreign commerce consists in the imports by which a country obtains a more ample supply of the commodity it wants for the same labour and capital or the same supply for less labour and capital, leaving the surplus disposable to produce other things. The vulgar theory that regards the advantage of commerce as residing in the exports is a relic of the Mercantile Theory (*supra*, § 2 A), and even Adam Smith, who destroyed this Theory, made a mistake in considering that the benefit of foreign trade was in affording an outlet for the surplus produce of a country. No country is under the necessity of producing what it exports; it only produces it as the cheapest mode of supplying itself with other things. And if prevented from exporting the surplus in any particular commodity, the labour and capital employed in producing this surplus would find employment in producing those things which had been previously imported by means of the surplus. The profits of the merchant engaged in foreign commerce might be equally great if he employed his Capital in production at home. To suppose the contrary would be to fall into the error that there can be such a thing as over-production (*supra*, § 37 A).

(ii) Indirect.

(*a*) Economical. Every extension of the market improves processes of production by more extended division of labour, greater use of machinery, etc. And also the opening of a foreign trade increases the people's tastes and desires, and may thus work an industrial revolution in stimulating their energy and ambition.

(*b*) Intellectual and Moral. Commerce provides valuable communication between the civilised nations and is the principle guarantee of the peace of the world [!].

40. International Values.

A. *The Problem Stated.* The values of commodities exchanged in the same place or in adjacent places between which Capital moves freely depend, temporary fluctuations apart, upon their Cost of Production. On what does the value of a commodity brought from a foreign country depend? It depends on its cost of acquisition in the place to which it is brought, and this means *the cost of production of the thing which is exported to pay for it.* In this way does cost of production affect international values; but it does not finally determine them, as an example will show. Suppose ten yards of cloth equal fifteen yards of linen in England and twenty yards of linen in Germany. If England buys twenty yards of linen in Germany with ten yards of cloth she will clearly have gained five yards of linen by the exchange, and Germany will be no better off. If, on the other hand, England buys fifteen yards of linen at the same cost, Germany will be five yards of linen to the good and England will have no advantage. For both to gain, the amount of linen to be given by Germany for ten yards of cloth must be somewhere between fifteen and twenty yards.

N.B.—An example of barter like this is appropriate to international trade, which is always, in reality, an actual trucking of one commodity against another.

B. *The Equation of International Demand.* Now a special version of the law of cost of production has enabled us to fix the two extremes between which the international values may oscillate. What determines the actual terms of international exchange on which the value depends? To explain this we must have recourse to the other Law of Value: that of Supply and Demand. If England demands linen more than Germany demands cloth, she will only get say sixteen yards of linen for ten of cloth; but if Germany wants cloth more than England wants linen, Germany will have to pay, say eighteen yards of linen for ten of cloth. Thus the terms of international exchange depend on *the Equation of International Demand*.

How is this affected.

(i) By cost of Carriage? This makes things dearer in the place to which they are imported by the amount of the cost, which is not, however, necessarily paid by each importing country nor divided between the two countries in the ratio of the advantage which each gains. It would always depend upon the play of international demand whether the producing or the importing country would most benefit if the cost of carriage could be annihilated. If there were no cost of carriage and the trade were free, every commodity would be either regularly imported or regularly exported. But cost of carriage limits exportation, especially of bulky articles.

(ii) By more than two commodities? This will render the illustration of the Law of International Values more complicated, but will not disturb it; it only adds more elements to the calculation *e.g.* England's demand for linen from Germany, if not equalled by Germany's demand for cloth from England, might be equalled or surpassed by Germany's demand for cloth *and* iron from England.

(iii) By more than two countries? In this case the law still holds *e.g.* a third country is willing to give more yards of linen for England's cloth than Germany has been giving. This increase of demand will raise the value of England's cloth.

Thus the Law of International Values is but an extension of the Law of Supply and Demand (*supra*,

§ 29, ii. end) and the equation of International Demand may be concisely stated as follows:—

The products of a country are exchanged for the products of other countries at such values as are required in order that the whole of her exports may exactly pay for the whole of her imports.

C. The effect of an improvement in production on international values. If an improvement tends to cheapen the cost of producing a commodity, will the foreigner who imports the article get the benefit of this cheapening? To some extent no doubt, but to what extent will depend,

(i) On the side of the importing country, on whether the increase of demand for the cheaper commodity is in proportion to the cheapness or in greater or less proportion than it. The more the demand is increased, the less will be the benefit.

(ii) On the side of the producing country, on whether the incomes freed by the cheapening of one article set up an increased demand for the articles of foreign countries. The more this demand is increased the greater will be the benefit to the foreign countries.

[Mill's later additions to his Theory of International Values, Book III., Chap. 18 § 6—8, even if they are not, as they have been called "laborious and confusing" did not add much to his original exposition. He points out that International Values do not depend solely on the quantities demanded but also on the means of production available in each country for the supply of foreign markets. But he goes on to say that the practical result is little affected by this conditional element. For the Capital which a country has to spare from the production of domestic commodities for its own use is in proportion to the demand for foreign commodities. The chief consequence to be noted from this is that the richest countries gain the least by a given amount of foreign commerce, since, having the greater demand for commodities generally, they are likely to modify the terms of interchange to their own disadvantage.]

D. *Cost of foreign imports.* We have seen that an imported commodity is cheaper in *value* than such a commodity would be if produced at home to an extent that depends on the Laws of International Demand. It is also cheaper in *cost, i.e.,* a greater quantity of it can be obtained with the same expenditure of labour and capital. The extent of this cheapness will depend upon the cost of producing the commodity exported to pay for it. It follows therefore that every country gets its imports at *less cost in proportion to the general efficiency of its labour.*

41. Money as an Import.

Money may be imported into a country in two ways—

A. Simply as a commodity (chiefly in bullion) and

B. As a medium of exchange.

A. *As a commodity* money obeys the same Laws of Value as other imported commodities. To put it simply, the bullion exported from Brazil to England must exactly pay for the cottons or other English goods required by Brazil. The matter is of course more complicated than this, for the demand in all foreign countries for English products must be brought into equilibrium with the demand in England for the products, bullion among the rest, of foreign countries. Money will also be affected by cost of carriage in such a way that this Law of Value may be generally summarised as follows: the countries in which money will be of least value, or, in other words, in which prices will habitually range the highest, are those

(i) Whose exportable productions are most in demand abroad, and

(ii) Contain greatest value in smallest bulk (to lessen cost of transport),

(iii) Which are nearest to the mines, and

(iv) Which have least demand for foreign productions.

Moreover the cost of money is cheaper where industry is most efficient. This is why money is obtained at less cost by England than by most countries. It is doubtful whether it is also of less *value*, *i.e.*, whether prices are high in England compared with other countries, but if it be so this must be occasioned by (i) and (ii).

It has been contended that the value of money must depend exclusively on its cost of production at the mines. This is not so, for any circumstances which disturb the equation of demand in a country must affect the value of money in that country. Thus an increase in the foreign demand for English products will enable England to get all her commodities, and bullion among the rest, on cheaper terms; nor need this demand come from the mining countries. England might export nothing to them and yet might obtain bullion from them on the lowest terms through an intensity of demand in other foreign countries, which would pay circuitously with gold and silver from the mining countries. For the *whole of its exports* are what a country exchanges against the *whole of its imports*, and not simply the exports and imports to and from any one country.

B. *As a medium of exchange* money is sent from one country to another generally for the payment of goods, and to understand when and why it passes from country to country for this purpose it is necessary to explain the mechanism of the foreign exchanges. The habitual mode of payment for commodities between country and country is by

(i) Bills of Exchange (*supra*, § 38 B).

An Englishman, A, consigns goods to a Frenchman, B, while another Englishman, C, receives goods of equal value from a Frenchman, D. A draws a bill on B, C buys this bill from A and sends it to D, who gets the money from B. Thus the transaction is completed without any money passing from England to France. This illustration supposes the sum of debts due from one country to another to be equal. If there is a greater sum due from England to France than is due from France to England, or *vice versa*, the debts cannot simply be written off against one another. After the one has been applied as far as it will go towards covering the other the balance must be transmitted in the precious metals.

(ii) The business of buying and selling Bills in each country is done by brokers, and if a broker finds that he is asked for Bills on one place to a greater amount than Bills on another he does not, on this account, refuse to give them, but asks in addition to the Bills a price sufficient to cover freight and insurance for transmitting the precious metals, together with the profit. Buyers are willing to pay this premium rather than go to the expense of remitting the metal themselves. On the other hand, if brokers have more Bills than are wanted, such Bills fall to a discount and, through competition, the brokers have to give the benefit of this discount to those who buy the Bills for purposes of remittance.

(iii) In our illustration above the exchange between England and France is *at par*, *i.e.*, a Bill on France for £100 would sell for exactly £100. If, however, England had a larger sum to pay to France than to receive from her, the Bill on France for £100 would sell for more than £100 and Bills would be said to be *at a premium*; while if England had more to receive from France than to pay, a Bill on France for £100 would be bought for somewhat less than £100, and would be said to be *at a discount*.

(iv) When Bills on foreign countries are at a premium, it is customary to say that the exchanges are *against* the country *unfavourable* to it. The "exchange" means the power which the money of the country has of purchasing the money of other countries, and the phrase "unfavourable" (applied to it when a country has to pay a premium for the Bills it buys) is a relic of the old theory that the benefit of a trade consisted in bringing money into the country. As a matter of fact, when Bills on France are at a premium in England only those suffer who have to pay money in France because they are buyers of Bills. Those who have money to receive in France get advantage of the premium as sellers of Bills.

(v) Now the variations in the exchanges are often *self-adjusting*. When Bills are at a premium it means that money has to be exported, owing to the fact that a greater money value of goods has been imported than exported, but the premium itself is an extra gain for the exporters and a diminution of profit to those who import. Thus an encouragement is given to exportation, which often increases to such an extent that a merely casual disturbance in the ordinary course of trade between two countries is soon liquidated in commodities and the account adjusted by means of Bills without the transmission of bullion.

(vi) On the other hand excess of imports over exports may arise from a *permanent cause*, viz., the state of prices. In such a case the condition can only be rectified through prices, either the subtraction of actual money from the circulation of one of the countries or the annihilation of credit equivalent to it.

N.B.—Exchanges do not depend on the balance of debts and credits with each country *separately*, but of *all countries taken together, e.g.*, England may by what is called "arbitration of exchange," liquidate a balance of payments to France with Bills on Holland, which owes her a balance.

42. International Distribution of the Precious Metals.

The Laws of international values were arrived at on the hypothesis of *barter*, but the intervention of money and its substitutes makes no difference. This is quite clearly the case when the exports and imports of countries exactly balance one another or are, in the language of mechanics, in a condition of stable equilibrium.

When, however, the equation of international demand

is not established between two countries, is the process of restoring it a different thing in a money system to what it is in a barter system? It must first of all be remembered that the introduction of money is a mere addition of one more commodity. Then the method by which the equation of international demand is established is as follows: Money goes out of a country to pay an adverse balance, and even if this money is at first paid out of hoards, and therefore does not affect prices by leaving the country, it must eventually be paid out of circulating money, because only a change of prices will establish the equation. When the circulating money begins to go prices will fall in the country which has to export the money, and in consequence of the lower prices a greater demand will grow up for that country's commodities until the equation of demand and supply has at length been reached. This was exactly what we noted on the supposition of barter. In a barter system the trade gravitates to the point at which the sum of the imports exactly exchanges for the sum of the imports; in a money system it gravitates to the point at which the sum of the imports and the sum of the exports exchanges for the same quantity of money.

Similarly if we examine the effect of an improvement in production in the light of money values between different countries we shall arrive at exactly the same conclusions as we did in examining it on the supposition of barter (*supra*, § 40 C). We can thus sum up our conclusions with regard to the distribution of precious metals in the following words of Ricardo: "Gold and silver having been chosen for the general medium of circulation, they are, by the competition of commerce, distributed in such proportions amongst the different countries of the world as to accommodate themselves to the natural traffic which would take place if no such metals existed, and the trade between countries were purely a trade of barter."

Nor does this use of money as a medium of exchange alter in the least the law of the value of the precious metals themselves. The causes which bring money into or carry it out of a country through the exchanges are the very causes on which the local value of money would depend if it were never imported except as merchandise and never except directly from the mines; viz., changes in the international demand for commodities. When money flows from country to country in consequence of these changes, and so alters its own local value, it merely realises, by a more rapid process, the effect which would otherwise take place more slowly.

N.B.—Money may pass from country to country as tribute, remittances of rent to absentee landlords, interest to foreign creditors, etc. In such cases the paying country loses not only what it pays, but, having an excess of exports over imports, has also to offer its commodities, to make up the exports, on cheaper terms or pay dearer for foreign commodities, and so loses something else in addition to what it has to pay.

43. Influence of Currency on Foreign Trade.

The value of the precious metals depends on the general laws of the value of imported commodities, and affects trade between other countries and the mining countries according to those general laws. But casual and temporary variations in the value of money may also produce effects on international trade.

A. Effect of a sudden increase of currency. The bringing into circulation of hoards of treasure, or the sudden creation of bank notes or other substitutes for money, would have the immediate effect of raising prices. This would check exports and encourage imports. The exchanges would become unfavourable and money would flow out of the country until the difference were only such as had existed before, the only difference being that in the case of the sudden creation of bank notes or the like, since a smaller annual supply of precious metals will now be required, there will be some disturbance in the equilibrium of payments between the mining countries and the rest of the world. But there would also be another effect when the paper money was introduced. Suppose the creation in England of bank notes to the amount of twenty million pounds. Twenty millions which formerly existed in the unproductive form of metallic money would, by going out of England to pay for exports, have been converted into what is, or is capable of becoming, productive Capital. In fact the substitution of paper in the room of precious metals has been compared by Adam Smith to the construction of a highway through the air, by which the ground now occupied by roads would become available for agriculture. Of course this depends upon how the new twenty millions is used. If used by the Government for paying off debt, or if supplied by bankers or banking companies, it will probably become productive Capital. If squandered uselessly by the Government, or made the substitute for mere temporary taxation, it may be unproductive. That it can, however, be productively employed is a great argument for the substitution of paper for the precious metals, whenever it can be made with safety, *i.e.*, whenever a sufficient amount of metallic currency is retained to maintain, both in fact and in public belief, the convertibility of the paper.

B. Effect of the Increase of an Inconvertible Paper Currency. When an inconvertible paper currency begins to exceed in quantity the metal currency which it supersedes, prices will rise, and this rise of prices will not, as in A, stimulate imports, because imports and exports are determined by metallic prices and not paper prices; and it is only when the paper is exchangeable at pleasure with metals that paper prices and metallic prices must correspond. A depreciation of the currency therefore does not affect the foreign trade of a country; it does, however, affect the exchanges, *e.g.*, the imports and exports between France and England are in equilibrium and metallic currency would be at par. But inconvertible paper in England has made £5 of gold cost £6; thus, while the real exchange between England and France is

£5 for £5 in gold, the nominal exchange shows that a Bill on France for £5 will be worth £6. But however high this nominal premium may be, it has no tendency to send gold out of the country for the purpose of drawing a Bill against it and profiting by the premium, because the gold so sent must be procured, not from the banks and at par as in the case of convertible currency, but in the market at an advance in price equal to the premium.

44. Rate of Interest.

A. The general law of Interest (*supra*, § 26 A (i)). Interest is really a question of exchange value, since it is paid for loans and is connected with the phenomena of what is erroneously called the money market. Now the real rate of interest at any time (*i.e.*, leaving out of consideration insurance against risk) depends upon there being people anxious to borrow at the same rate as others are willing to lend, *i.e.*, it depends upon the supply and demand of loans. Now this demand and supply fluctuates more excessively than any other, but it is possible to discover some, more or less permanent, rate.

(i) The circumstances that determine the permanent demand and supply of loans must be discovered where commerce is in a quiescent condition. In such circumstances the demand for loans would be from producers and traders with their own capital fully employed, or from government and land owners and other unproductive consumers with good security. Now to supply this demand there may be many people with more Capital than they are themselves inclined to use or qualified for using. If the mass of Capital in such hands was greater than the demand, interest would bear a low proportion of the rate of profit and so borrowers would be tempted to borrow more than they needed, or lenders would be discouraged from lending. If, on the other hand, the mass was short of the habitual demand for loans, the rate of interest would be raised so high as to re-establish the equilibrium.

Now the lending of money need not be done merely by those not in business, but may be a business in itself in the hands of others—

(*a*) Professional money-lenders, who will, however, require for their loans, in addition to interest, profits and insurance against risk, and will not therefore be dealt with by borrowers for the purpose of business since they cannot afford to pay the full profit for that for which they will themselves receive no more, and

(*b*) Bankers, etc., who are able to lend, not merely their own capital, but also their credit, *i.e.*, the capital of other persons. And it is the amount in the hands of bankers (which, being lent for short times only, is continually in the market seeking investments) that is one of the chief

(ii) Circumstances which determine the fluctuations in the rate of interest. The *supply* of Capital is liable to variation according to the amount in the hands of bankers, though it is less liable than the demand. At the beginning of a period of speculation all lenders are inclined to extend their business by stretching their credit, and accordingly these are times when the rate of interest is low. During the revulsion interest rises inordinately because of the pressing need of borrowers and the general disinclination to lend, which when it is at its extreme point is called a panic. In the intervals between commercial crises there is usually a tendency in the rate of interest to a progressive decline from the general process of accumulation. Other causes which affect supply are

(*a*) Gold discoveries, which tend to lower interest.

(*b*) Growth of limited liability companies, which tend to draw capital from the loan market and so to raise interest.

(*c*) Greater willingness to send Capital abroad, which also tends to raise interest at home.

Demand for loans causes greater variations; it arises from—

(*a*) Wars: when the Government generally incurs new loans, which succeed each other rapidly as long as the war lasts.

(*b*) The sudden opening of new and attractive modes of permanent investment, *e.g.*, railways.

B. Connection of Interest with the *Value of Money*. As a general rule money is only the medium by which capital or commodities pass. But

(i) Sometimes a loan is wanted, not as capital, but as money to meet a debt. This is particularly the case in a commercial crisis. Yet though money alone is wanted in such cases, capital passes, and if loans are made freely at a time of commercial crisis it may be said with truth that it is by an addition to loanable capital that the rise of the rate of interest is met and corrected.

(ii) The quantity or value of money in circulation makes no difference to the rate of interest. A permanent depreciation of the currency may diminish the power of money to buy commodities, but not the power of money to buy money. If £100 will buy a perpetual annuity of £4 a year, a depreciation which makes the £100 worth only half as much as before has precisely the same effect on the £4. Yet

(iii) A change of a less quantity to a greater quantity of money or from a greater to a less may and does make a difference in it. If money is in process of depreciation by means of inconvertible currency, the demand for real capital on loan will not be diminished. But the capital loanable, since it exists only as money which has been depreciated, will be diminished, and so the rate of interest must rise. The reverse will happen as the effect of calling in a depreciated currency. On the other hand the introduction of additional gold and silver or a paper currency like that of England which goes into the loan market will add to the amount of loanable capital and can only get itself invested by lowering the rate of interest.

On the whole then loans as money are of less importance than loans as real capital. The exaggerated importance that is sometimes given to the money aspect arises, among other things, from the use of the phrase "the value of money" to designate the rate of interest, when it really means the purchasing power of the circulating medium (*supra*, § 33 C). An unfortunate result of this misconception has been to lead people in times of crisis to pay too much attention to the effect produced by banks by their issues of notes, and to pay too little attention to their management of their deposits, means of which they more frequently make imprudent by extensions of credit.

C. *Prices* determined by the Rate of Interest. The current rate of interest affects the price of public funds and all description of securities. They are sold at the price which will give the market rate of interest on the purchase money, with allowance for differences in the rate of the risk incurred, etc. The price of land, mines and other fixed sources of income depends in like manner on the rate of interest. Land usually sells at a higher price (in proportion to the income it affords) than the public funds, because it is thought to be more secure and ideas of powers and dignity are connected with it. When interest is low land will be dearer and *vice versa*, though both the price of land and the rate of interest happened to be high during the Napoleonic wars owing to the continuance of a very high average price of corn for many years.

45. The Regulation of a Convertible Paper Currency.

A. There are *two contrary theories* on this subject, which may be summed up as follows—

> I. The Banking Theory. "We are willing to consider a metallic currency as the type of that to which a mixed circulation of coin and paper ought to conform, but further we contend that it has so conformed and must so conform while the paper is strictly convertible."

II. The Currency Theory. That the issue of notes beyond what is necessary raises prices and so generates speculation, and thus finally produces commercial crises.

I. The upholders of the banking theory deny to convertible banknotes any power of raising prices, and use the following line of argument to show that the rise and fall of prices has always preceded the enlargement or contraction of bank circulation.

(i) In the *quiescent* state of the markets the extra issue of notes to meet the demands of an individual do not remain in circulation any more than the extra quantity of Bank of England notes issued once a quarter to pay dividends. They return on deposit.

(ii) Even in the *expectant* or speculative state of the market

(*a*) The increase of circulation always *follows* the rise of prices.

(*b*) Speculative purchases are not affected by bank notes, but by cheques or book credit.

(*c*) Even an issue of notes would, after being used for a specific purpose, return on deposit.

(*b*) and (*c*) are true so long as the period of circulation is confined to dealers.

But this is the point at which we arrive at the arguments for the Currency Theory.

II. When speculation has arrived so far as to reach the producers,

(i) Bank notes are wanted to pay wages, and these do not return on deposit. This was especially the case when £1 and £2 notes were permitted by law.

(ii) Unsuccessful speculators demand advances to hold on: this exhausts loanable Capital: the bank over-issues notes: thus the period of speculation is artificially prolonged: precious metals are exported: the bank finds it difficult to meet the payment of its notes and a crisis ensues.

B. The currency theorists triumphed in the *Bank Charter Act* of 1844. The chief points of which are:—

(i) The Bank of England may issue notes to the value of fifteen million pounds without specie basis. Notes above this must have a specie reserve, of which one-fifth may be silver.

(ii) The issue department is separated from the banking department.

(iii) No London bank nor any bank chartered since 1844 could issue notes, and the issue of English banks then existing was limited to the outstanding circulation before 1844.

I. *In favour of* the Act it may be said that, although there is nothing in it to prevent banks from having recourse, in times of exceptional demand for advances to their deposit account (as the Bank of England did in 1847), yet the limitation of the increase of issues does prevent them from accelerating or aggravating the crisis.

II. The general argument *against* the Act is that it limits the currency of a country.

(i) It limits the powers of the bank to restore credit in the collapse that follows a crisis; so that it has to be suspended in such cases, as it was in 1847 and 1857.

(ii) The drain of gold does not merely arise from speculation. It may also arise from—

(*a*) Extraordinary foreign expenditure.

(*b*) Large exportation of Capital for foreign investment.

(*c*) Failure of crops of raw materials in other countries.

(*d*) Bad harvest and great consequent importation of food.

In such cases harm rather than good is done by anything that tends to limit the currency, because the amount of available Capital is needlessly exhausted, the hoards of gold being at the bank, not, as in many other countries, in different hands. A drain in the banking department of three millions means a limitation of three millions in the issue department. And thus, by the double action of drains, the three millions equals six millions.

(iii) In such cases, to replenish its reserve, the bank must have recourse to high rates of interest. Therefore contractions of credit are made more severe and more frequent by the Act.

To make the Act innocuous the bank should retain, plus its reserve in the issue department, as great a reserve in gold or notes in the banking department alone as would suffice under the old system for the security of both issues and deposits.

C. Should the issue of bank notes be confined to a *single establishment?* The gain is so enormous (practically 100%) that if there is to be a monopoly the nation should share it; not, perhaps, by the Government undertaking the issue, but by a loan without interest from an establishment like the Bank of England of fifteen or twenty million notes. One body should be made responsible for maintaining a reserve of precious metals sufficient to meet a reasonable drain either

(i) By confining the issue to one body, or

(ii) By making one body pay in gold and permitting the other to pay in the notes of the central body.

A dissemination of responsibility prevents it from operating efficiently in any one establishment.

N.B.—If plurality of issuers be allowed, the holders of notes should be specially protected against failure of payment.

46. Underselling.

One of the chief aims and objects of countries under the Mercantile System was to undersell one another, as if production and commodities existed for no other purpose. Now that we realise that it is the commodities bought, and not the commodities sold, which are of chief importance in foreign trade, we are not inclined to lay so much stress on the problem of underselling, but still the competition of different countries in the same market is a matter of some importance, because the commodities sold are a means of obtaining those which are bought.

A. What then are the causes which enable one country to undersell another? There are only two conditions on which one country can entirely expel another from a given market.

(i) She must have a greater advantage than the second country in the production of the article for export.

(ii) She must have such relations with the customer country as to be able to give her more than the whole advantage possessed by the rival country in respect of the international exchange.

A mere diminution of advantage will not be sufficient to drive out a rival, and it is possible for the alarm of being permanently undersold to be taken much too easily. Suppose, for example, a rival underselling English cloth in the foreign markets. This may cause a diminution of exports from England and a new distribution of the precious metals with the resulting fall in prices, with the result that England may again be able to compete with her rivals.

Now besides greater natural advantages, better division of labour, or superior capability in the labourers, *one* of the contributory factors to (i) may be low wages, which is what, according to current theories, is the main, if not the only, cause of underselling.

B. Low wages are certainly *one* of the causes of underselling, but not to the extent that is usually supposed. In the first place it is not the wages themselves that are of importance, but the Cost of Labour. High wages do not always mean a high

Cost of Labour because the higher paid labourer may work longer and be more efficient. But low wages, even in the sense of low Cost of Labour, only enable a country to undersell when peculiar to certain branches of industry, for then the comparative cost of production of those articles in relation to others is lessened. The case is similar with domestic manufactures produced in the leisure hours of families, partially occupied in other pursuits, but no such advantage is conferred by low wages when common to all branches of industry. For, as we have seen (*supra*, § 30, 3 (ii)), general low wages do not cause low prices any more than high wages cause high prices. It is quite true that a country whose general Cost of Labour is low can undersell in a foreign market a country whose general Cost of Labour is higher and still get as high a profit as the rival country, but the merchant of that country will expect to get as high profits as the other merchants of *his own* country; not as the merchants of the country with the high Cost of Labour, where the average rate of profits will be low.

N.B.—Some countries, *e.g.*, the West Indies, are not to be looked upon as separate countries for the purposes of commerce, but rather as outlying establishments belonging to a larger community. In them the rate of profit will be regulated by the rate of the country whence they get their capital. Other countries, *e.g.*, Venice and the Hanse Towns, have supported themselves by a mere carrying trade without any productions of their own. They made themselves and their Capital instruments, not of production, but of accomplishing exchanges between the productions of other countries. This was because these other countries had not Capital disposable for this operation. When, however, the Capital of these other countries increased, competition arose in the carrying trade, which passed to other countries, *e.g.*, Holland, which could afford to work for small profit.

47. How Exchange affects Distribution.

We must now consider whether the laws which regulate the three-fold division of the produce are affected by the machinery of exchange.

(i) Wages depend on the ratio between population and Capital, and wages (*i.e.*, real wages, or wages in kind, that is to say, wages in the sense in which they are of importance to the receiver) in any country are habitually at the lowest rate to which, in that country, the labourer will suffer them to be depressed rather than put a restraint upon multiplication. Money wages, *i.e.*, wages in the sense in which they are of importance to the payer, do not depend upon such simple principles. They are compounded of two elements—

(*a*) Real wages, or the quantity which the labourer obtains of the ordinary articles of consumption.

(*b*) The money prices of those articles.

Now the money price of food depends upon the cost of production of the food which is grown in the least advantageous circumstances, and it is the pressure of population that forces less and less fertile lands into cultivation. Therefore the same cause operates on money wages as operates on real wages, and exchange and money make no difference in the law of wages.

(ii) Land on the extreme margin of cultivation affords a measure of rent. Now the price of food will always on the average be such that the worst land shall just replace the expenses with ordinary profit; the extra profit on better lands becomes the prize of the landlords. Exchange and money, therefore, make no difference in the law of rent.

(iii) Profits form the surplus of the produce after replacing wages and paying rent, therefore exchange and money can make no difference in the law of profits.

[48. The Dynamics of Political Economy.

In Book iv. Mill deals with the progressive changes in the economical condition of mankind, and as his remarks are largely of a prophetic nature and have in some cases been falsified by time, it is only necessary—and that for the sake of completeness—to summarize them briefly. Starting from the hypothesis that Society tends to progress towards increased command over the powers of nature, increased security, and increased capacity of co-operation, he points out that the result is a tendency to a decline of *the value and cost* of the production of all commodities except those subject to the direct operation of the law of diminishing returns, which have a tendency to rise unless the tendency is counteracted by improvements in production, but that increased facilities of communication and the operations of speculative dealers tend to moderate fluctuations of value. (The speculator, even the corn-dealer, does not make high prices but mitigates them.) With regard to the influence of progress on *rents, profits and wages*, Mill notes the results in a variety of cases according as to which of the three features of industrial progress, increase of capital, increase of population, or improvements in production, either taken separately, in pairs, or all together, is in operation, and comes to the conclusion that the general tendency is for the cost of the labourer's subsistence to increase, for profits to fall, and for rents to rise enormously, and that, even if agricultural improvements counteract the first two tendencies, they will only temporarily check the rise of rents, which will eventually be greatly increased by such improvements. [The fall of rents during the last half century hardly bears out Mill's contentions]. With regard to falling of profits, Mill points out that they tend to *fall to a minimum*, that minimum being the lowest amount which in any given Society, according to the strength of the effective desire of accumulation and of security of Capital industrially employed, will induce men to save rather than to spend. The reaching of that minimum in opulent countries is only prevented by the waste of capital in periods of rash speculation, by improvements in production which have the effect of extending the field of employment, by any new power of obtaining cheap commodities from foreign countries, and by the overflow of capital into foreign countries in search of higher profits. Mill draws two morals from his theory of the tendency of profits to a minimum (1) that in opulent countries the expenditure of public money for valuable, even though unproductive purposes, will not diminish the wages fund, (2) nor will, in such countries, the fixing of large quantities of capital in machinery, etc. ; for the abstraction of circulating capital by raising profits and interest, gives a fresh stimulus to accumulation.

Such are the effects of industrial progress, but what is its end ? A stationary state of wealth and population, which, says Mill, is not in itself undesirable, for a condition of struggle is not in itself an ideal, and in a stationary state there would be much more likelihood of the Art of Living being improved. Nor is there any need to suppose that the distribution of wealth and the division of classes will always be such as they now are. The theory of the dependence of the working classes is no longer applicable, and their future will depend on their better education, which will lead them to check the growth of population (especially if it is accompanied by the social and industrial independence of women); while the relation of hiring and service will tend to be discontinued and *Co-operation* (made more possible by legalization of limited liability companies) will take its place either in the form of associations of labourers with capitalists or of labourers among themselves. Such co-operation does not carry with it the elimination of competition, which the Socialists desire, forgetting that wherever competition is not, monopoly is; and that monopoly in all its forms is the taxation of the industrious for the support of indolence, if not of plunder. (Mill's hopes of Co-operation have not so far been borne out by its subesquent history, which has shown it developing on the lines rather of Distributive or Consumptive Co-operation, (*i.e.*, combination of consumers to buy goods at wholesale prices) than of Productive Co-operation).]

49. The Functions of Government.

These are either

A. Necessary, *i.e.*, such as are inseparable from the idea of a Government, such as raising the revenue, which is the condition of a Government's existence, the repression of force and fraud, etc., etc.

B. Optional, *i.e.*, overstepping the boundaries of the universally acknowledged functions. Some of these cases of governmental interference depend upon the influence of false general theories, others may be discovered on examination to be really advisable.

50. Taxation. General Principles.

A. Adam Smith's four maxims.

(i) The subjects of every State ought to contribute to the support of the Government as nearly as possible in proportion to their respective abilities.

(ii) The tax which each individual is bound to pay ought to be certain and not arbitrary.

(iii) Every tax ought to be levied at the time, or in the manner, in which it is most likely to be convenient for the contributor to pay it.

(iv) Every tax ought to be so contrived as both to take out and to keep out of the pockets of the people as little as possible over and above what it brings into the public treasury of the State.

(ii), (iii) and (iv) require no explanation, but (i) requires to be more fully examined.

B. The *equality of taxation* aimed at in Adam Smith's first maxim means equality of sacrifice; *i.e.*, apportioning the contribution of each person towards the expenses of government so that he shall feel neither more nor less inconvenience from his share in the payment than every other person experiences from his. If you assume that a man should pay in proportion to the amount of protection he receives from government, you may argue that the State in protecting property does twice as much for the man with £200 a year as for the man with £100 a year; and that therefore the former ought to pay twice as much as the latter. On the other hand you may argue that the State as protector of persons gives equal value to all men alike and that therefore a poll-tax is justifiable. It is, in fact, impossible to estimate the degrees of benefit which different persons derive from the protection of government. Thus the most satisfactory ground on which to rest the principle of equality of taxation is that of each man contributing according to his means. Granting this

C. How is *equal sacrifice* secured in different cases?

(i) Should the same percentage be levied on all amounts of income, or should there be a *graduated Income Tax?* The exemption of very small incomes may be admitted on the grounds that any tax on them would be a tax on the necessaries of life, whereas a tax of a similar percentage on higher incomes could be saved from luxuries. There should be an untaxed minimum fixed at an amount necessary for maintaining life, *e.g.*, suppose that minimum £50, an income of £50 would not be taxed at all, one of £60 would be taxed as if it were £10 and one of £1,000 as if it were £950. Further than this the arguments for graduated Income Tax (*l'impot progressif*) have no weight. It is impossible to say with any degree of certainty that the man with £10,000 a year cares less for £1,000 than the person with £1,000 cares for £100. It is no argument in favour of a graduated tax that it would be a means of mitigating the inequalities of wealth, for it would not be desirable to achieve this by laying a tax on industry and economy. A distinction might be made between earned and unearned incomes, and, by way of securing a fairer start for all, taxes, and even graduated taxes, might be placed on inheritances and legacies.

A special tax on *realised property*, *i.e.*, property not part of any capital employed by its owner is even more objectionable than a graduated Property Tax, for it taxes only a small part of the community, and the whole weight of the tax would fall on those persons who composed that class when the tax was first imposed; for it would cause a reduction of price in land, the public funds and other securities in which "realised property" was invested equivalent to the amount of the tax, and so when the holders of these securities came to sell them they would find that their capital had diminished to an extent proportional to the tax.

(ii) Should the same percentage be levied on *Perpetual* and on *Terminable Incomes?* It seems manifestly unjust that the person whose income dies with him should pay the same amount as the man who can transmit his, undiminished, to his descendants. Yet, arithmetically, there is no violation of the rule of proportion, for the terminable income only pays for the period it exists. The perpetual income pays it theoretically in perpetuity. The grounds on which the temporary annuitant has a claim are not those of smaller means but of greater necessities; he usually has more demands on his income, and it is usually necessary for him to save for his children or for his own old age. Such savings at any rate should, where possible, be exempted, for they pay not only income tax as income, but also income tax on the interest they receive as capital. To exempt savings would not be to disturb the natural competition between the motives for saving and those for spending. It is rather the taxing of them which disturbs this natural competition. But how would it be possible to arrange a form for income tax returns under which savings were to be exempted of which fraudulent advantage would not be taken? It would, therefore, be best to make an arbitrary distinction between perpetual and terminable incomes and exempt, *e.g.*, a fourth of the latter, from taxation.

Thus in interpreting the maxim of equality of taxation we must consider, not what people have, but what they can afford to spend, and try to make the tax proportionate to the latter.

D. In some cases *exceptions* may be made to equality of taxation without violating equal justice. Rent tends to increase with the ordinary progress of society; landlords grow richer as it were in their sleep, without work, risk, or economising. What claim have they, on the general principle of social justice, to this accession of riches? A valuation of all the land in the country, followed up by a general tax on increase of value afterwards, would be unjust to no one. [Mills idea was adopted in principle in the Finance Act of 1910, from which, however, agricultural land, which Mill expected to increase particularly in value, was exempted. A tax of 20% on the future unearned increment in the value of non-agricultural land, and a tax of $\frac{1}{2}$d. in the £ on the capital value on undeveloped land were imposed.] The existing Land Tax (1848) ought not to be regarded as a tax, but as a rent-charge in favour of the public, a portion of the rent, reserved from the beginning by the State, which has never belonged to or formed part of the income of the landlords, and could not therefore be counted to them as part of their taxation so as to exempt them from their fair share of every other tax.

E. It is sometimes laid down as a rule of taxation that it should fall *on income and not on Capital*. In so far as this means that there should not be over-taxation, which encroaches on the amount of the national Capital, this is a sound rule. But it is impossible to provide that taxes should fall entirely on income and not at all on Capital, for there is no tax which is not partly paid from what would otherwise have been saved, and in a country where Capital abounds and the spirit of accumulation is strong the effect of taxation on Capital is scarcely felt. Thus it is no objection to taxes on legacies that they are taxes on Capital, especially in a country like England, which has a national debt, because the produce of the tax thus applied to pay off the debt remains Capital, and is merely a transfer from the taxpayer to the fund-holder, and, moreover, in a country rapidly increasing in wealth the small amount of Capital abstracted in this way would only induce the saving of what would not otherwise be saved, or of what would otherwise be sent abroad for investment. (*Supra*, § 48).

51. Direct Taxes.

A direct tax = one which is demanded from the very persons who it is intended or desired should pay it. They are levied either on

    A. Income.
- (i) Rent,
- (ii) Profits,
- (iii) Wages, or
- (iv) All three sources of income, or on

    B. Expenditure, *i.e.*, such taxes on expenditure as fall immediately on the consumer, *e.g.*, a house tax.

Most other taxes on expenditure are indirect.

    A. (i) A tax on rent falls wholly on the landlord, *i.e.*, if it is a tax merely on true rent. If it falls also on what the tenant pays the landlord for capital improvements on the land it may tend to discourage such improvements, and therefore it would be well if that proportion of the nominal rent which may be regarded as landlord's profits were exempted from such a tax.

[An attempt is made to effect this in the present land taxes.]

(ii) A tax on profits falls in its immediate operation wholly on the payer. But it must be remembered that in a rich and prosperous country profits are always tending to a minimum (*supra*, § 48), and if the curtailment of profit produced by the tax is not counterbalanced by improvements in production it will tend either to check further accumulation or to cause a greater proportion of Capital than before to be sent abroad, *i.e.*, the minimum of profits will have been reached artificially before it would have been reached by the natural increase of Capital, and the effect will be to throw the burden of the tax on the labourer and the landlord, who would have benefitted by the extension of the Capital which the tax has prevented.

This is thought to have been the principal cause of the decline of Holland.

(iii) The incidents of a tax on wages varies according as the wages taxed are

(*a*) those of ordinary unskilled labour, or

(*b*) those of skilled or privileged employments.

(*b*) would fall directly on those taxed and the money would not, as has been argued, have come back to the labourers in increased demand for commodities; otherwise it might be argued the more Government takes in taxes generally the greater will be the demand for labour and the more opulent the condition of the labourers. The tax on (*a*) would at first fall on the labourers, but if their wages were regulated by an habitual standard of living, and that were not permanently lowered, the increase of population would receive a check and wages would rise. In that case the tax would fall, not on consumers generally as Adam Smith thought, since the rise of wages would not raise general prices, but on the producers, *i.e.*, it would fall on profits. This is an additional argument against a tax on very small incomes, a tax which will either degrade the habits of the labouring class or will fall on profits with the disadvantages detailed in (ii).

(iv) The general income tax fulfilling the conditions of § 49 C (i) and (ii) would be the least exceptionable of all taxes, the chief objection to it being the impossibility of ascertaining the real income of the contributors, for the main reliance has to be placed on the returns made by the person himself, and with regard to this only flagrant cases of falsehood can be detected. This objection would not be met by making the tax, not on income, but

B. On expenditure. Such a tax, *if general*, would still have to be ascertained from the statements of the contributors, and it is no more easy to judge of the known expenditure of most families from external signs than it is to judge of their incomes. Special taxes of this nature, such as horses, carriages, dogs and servants can be and are made use of, and do fall on the persons taxed.

A house tax is a tax of a similar description. If this is levied on the gross rent it falls

(i) both on the building rent, *i.e.*, on the ordinary profit for the labour and capital expended on the building,

(ii) and on the ground rent, which is determined by the ordinary principles of rent.

The tax on (i) falls on the consumer, *i.e.*, the occupier, though it might for a time fall on the owners of houses because the consumers might not be willing to pay their former rent, with the tax in addition, and so houses would be in excess of demand, and the supply of so durable a commodity could not quickly accommodate itself to the new circumstances.

The tax on (ii) might be expected to fall on the landlord, but would not wholly do so unless there were an equivalent tax on agricultural rent. Such portion of a house tax as falls on the ground landlord is liable to no valid objection, because in the only cases where it is of any considerable amount it is due to the accidental increase of site values in particular places through which enormous accessions of riches are acquired rapidly without exertion or outlay. And in so far as it falls on the occupier, the tax, if justly proportioned to the value of the house, and if houses below a certain value and business premises are exempted, is one of the fairest and most unobjectionable of all taxes, for no part of a person's expenditure is a better criterion of his means. Most local taxes are raised in this manner. The Window Tax was a House Tax of a bad kind, operating as a tax on light, and a cause of deformity in building.

52. Indirect Taxes.

Indirect taxes = those which are demanded from one person in the expectation and intention that he shall indemnify himself at the expense of another. Such are, as a rule, taxes on commodities when levied on production within the country or on importation into it or on conveyance or sale within, and known respectively as excise customs, tolls and transit duties. The effects of such taxes are—

(i) A tax on all commodities would fall on profits, because there would neither be a general rise of values, which is an absurdity, nor of prices, which depend on entirely different causes.

(ii) A tax on particular commodities, whether on a given quantity or *ad valorem*, will raise the price of the commodity by the amount of the tax, and generally by a bit more, owing to the frequent restrictions which interfere with the manufacture and also owing to the larger Capital required by the person who advances the tax and the tendency of the tax to limit the number of persons engaged in the business. In fine, the tax falls on the consumer in the form of an additional price, generally greater than the amount of the tax, and this usually occasions a lower demand for the commodity and, in consequence, an obstruction to improvements in production.

(iii) Since the values of the necessaries of the labourer have an influence on distribution, taxes on such commodities will have peculiar effects.

(*a*) A tax on corn will raise its price. What will result? Either the condition of the labouring classes will be lowered (and this is certain for a time at least) or the wages of the labourer will be made up by the employers to meet the increased expenses for food and the tax will come to be a peculiar tax on *profits*. Such a tax will not affect *rent* measured in any other commodity than corn; that is unless the tax be of sufficiently long standing to be affected by the tendency of profits to a minimum. If, through the operation of this tendency, the effect of the tax is to check accumulation, before such a check would come in the natural course of events, and if population is checked through the same cause, the tax will begin to affect rents. And the effect will become greater and greater with the lapse of time.

(*b*) Suppose a commodity to be capable of being made of two different processes, *e.g.*, sugar from the sugar-cane and from beetroot, and that a tax is laid on one and no tax, or a smaller one, on the other; if it taxes the worse of the two processes such a tax is simply nugatory, if the better it creates an artificial motive for preferring an inferior process and thus causes a waste of capital and labour, which adds to the price of the commodity and thus falls on the consumers. A discriminating duty, therefore, transgresses that rule of taxes, § 50 A (iv), that as little as possible should be taken from the taxpayer beyond what is brought into the treasury of the State. A tax on the importation of an article capable of being produced at home, *e.g.*, the Corn Laws, is a discriminating duty.

(v) Duties on exports and imports affect the equation of international demand. Such taxes are not wholly paid by the consumer. Thus a tax on our *exports* might, indeed, be wholly paid by the foreigner, but it might also be partly borne by ourselves. For if the increase of price is such as to cause a falling off in the demand of the foreigner the equation of international demand will be affected to our disadvantage and part of the tax will be paid indirectly by the consumer of the article imported to pay for the exported article. Conversely a tax on *imports*, if not sufficient for the purposes of protection (*i.e.*, so as to cause the article to be produced at home), might fall partly upon the foreigner, though such a gain is taken, not from the foreign producer but from the foreign consumer, who buys the article we export to pay for the taxed import. If such a tax leads to a retaliatory duty imposed by the foreigner, taxed things would be as before and each country would pay its own tax, unless the sum of the two duties exceeded the entire advantage of the trade which, in that case, would cease entirely.

53. Miscellaneous Taxes.

A. Taxes on contracts, which are usually levied by means of stamp duties and chiefly on purchases and sales,

(i) On consumable commodities, are simply taxes on the commodities and operate as described § 51.

(ii) On particular modes of sale, *e.g.*, auctions, operate to discourage such modes and fall on the seller, who is generally a necessitous person.

(iii) On land, are to be condemned as throwing an obstacle in the way of its sale and thus preventing the best use of the source of subsistence, and also as falling on the seller.

(iv) On leases, are pernicious, because, in a country of large property, leases are an essential condition of good agriculture.

(v) On insurance, are a direct discouragement to prudence.

B. Taxes on communication.

(i) On the conveyance of *letters*. If the charge for conveying letters be small the profits which the Government makes as the sole authorized carrier of them can hardly be considered as taxation, but rather as the profits of a business. The post office is one of the best of the sources from which this country derives its revenue. A charge in excess of what the postage would be in a system of freedom is an undesirable tax, acting like heavy tolls in increasing the expense of mercantile relations between distant places. Similar taxes on the communication of information are those

(ii) On *advertisements*, which, if too high, may prolong the period during which goods remain unsold, by preventing the coming together of the dealer and the consumer.

(iii). On *newspapers*, which fall on the chief sources of information of the largest and poorest part of the community.

C. Law Taxes are highly objectionable, for they do not, as has been argued, fall on those who benefit most by the law, but on those, who, being under the necessity of going to law, benefit least. They are a tax on redress and therefore a premium on injury.

D. Local Taxes should be levied for the specific purpose of local improvements, and should not be in excess of what is needed for that purpose. A toll on those who use a bridge or road may be levied until the capital expenditure of the construction has been raised; after which it should be thrown open and the expense of maintaining it laid on the locality in which it is situated. Local taxes are best raised as in England by direct taxation. Indirect taxation, like the octroi, either raises the prices of necessities coming from the country into the town, or, if wages rise to meet the increased cost of living, raises the prices of town produce since Capital will not remain in the town if its profits fall below their ordinary proportion as compared with the rural districts.

53. Direct v. Indirect Taxation.

A. Arguments

(i) For direct taxation.

(a) Everyone knows how much he really pays.

(b) Taxation being clearly perceived, there will be a security for economy in the public expenditure.

(ii) Against direct taxation.

(a) The puerile feeling of dislike, not so much to the paying as to the act of paying.

(b) Ignorance of the effect of indirect taxation diminishes daily. Moreover the fact that any ignorance still exists tells partially in favour of indirect taxation, because the same ignorance might not realise the necessity of certain expenditures which have to be defrayed out of taxation.

(c) Taxes on commodities are less burthensome than other taxes, because the contributor can escape from them by ceasing to use the taxed commodity. This is grounded on a fallacy. The taxpayer who consumed less wine in order to save £5 worth of tax on wine might equally consume less wine to save a direct tax of £5.

(d) The most valid argument for indirect taxation is that what is exacted is taken at a time and in a manner likely to be convenient to the payer.

(e) Direct taxation cannot be levied in sufficiently great quantities without conscientious co-operation on the part of the contributors, which is difficult to secure.

Thus while some revenue may be obtained from direct taxation, notably by land taxes, house taxes, legacy duties and (in a national emergency) income tax, the remainder must be levied by indirect taxation, and consequently we must ask

B. What forms of indirect taxation are most eligible? Excluding

> (i) Taxes which operate as protecting duties, and
>
> (ii) Taxes on the necessaries of life,

There remain taxes on *luxuries,* which, besides doing no one any harm, may even do good as a useful kind of sumptuary law. For raising such taxes the following practical rules may be laid down :—

> (i) To raise as much revenue as possible from those classes of luxuries which have most connection with *vanity* and least with positive enjoyment.
>
> (ii) To get the tax, when possible, direct from the *consumer* and not from the producer, since when it is got from the producer it always raises the price by more than the amount of the tax.
>
> (iii) Since the only indirect taxes which raise large amounts of revenue must be levied on luxuries of very general consumption, some *graduation* ought to be attempted in the tax, *e.g.,* the inferior kinds of tobacco ought to be taxed at a lower rate proportionately than the superior kinds.
>
> (iv) As *few* articles as possible should be taxed, in order that the expenses of collection be smaller and as few businesses as possible vexatiously interfered with.
>
> (v) The natural effect of a tax on a commodity is to check its consumption, therefore *stimulants* are a good object of such taxation, as being more liable than most other luxuries to be used in excess.
>
> (vi) A tax should be confined as far as possible to imported articles, because this entails less vexatious interference, *i.e., custom duties* are much less objectionable than excise, and should therefore be levied on things not producible or not allowed to be produced in the country.
>
> (vii) No tax ought to be so high as to furnish too strong a motive to its *evasion,* and so encourage smugglers, etc.

54. National Debt.

A. How far it is proper for a country to contract a debt, *i.e.*, not merely a temporary loan, as in the issue of exchequer bills payable in a year or two (a very convenient process when a Government does not possess a hoard), but of a permanent character? It is undesirable if the money so raised trenches on Capital which would otherwise be employed productively (*supra* § 9 C. end). And a very good test as to whether it is so trenching or not is the effect of such a loan on the current rate of interest. If it raises it, as during the Napoleonic wars, it is a positive proof that the Government is a competitor for Capital with the ordinary channels for productive investment, and could do no more harm if it actually raised the money by a direct tax on the labouring classes. When interest is not raised, the loans are limited to the overflow of the national Capital or the overflow of the general accumulation of the world, and it cannot be said then that the raising of money by loan is doing any direct harm. And though it is an excellent maxim to make present resources suffice for present wants, yet it may be reasonably held in a country increasing in wealth that its expenses will increase at the same ratio, and some of the cost of them therefore be distributed over the future.

B. Should such a debt be redeemed (i) at once by a general contribution, or (ii) gradually by a surplus revenue? (i) Would be best if it were practicable, and it would be practicable if it could justly be done by assessment on property alone, but only a certain amount would be justly due from persons with property. That amount they could easily pay and have the same net income as before. But persons with no accumulations, only incomes, could only make up by a single payment the equivalent of the annual charge of the tax by incurring a private debt equal to their share of the public debt, and it would be better for the debt to remain collective than to be parcelled out among individuals. For the debt is virtually a mutual insurance among the contributors. It is certainly desirable to maintain a surplus for paying off debt.

The argument that such money as is raised for this purpose should be left "to fructify in the pockets of the people" might have some weight with regard to taxes for unproductive expenditure, but has none whatever with regard to paying off a loan, because the fund-holders who are paid will presumably invest the money at once.

Before maintaining a surplus, however, it is probably best for a country to get rid of all its really bad taxes and even to reduce others as far as possible, eventually appropriating some particular tax, *e.g.*, succession duties, for the liquidation of the debt.

> *N.B.*—The argument that a national debt is desirable as an investment for the savings of the poor and inexperienced does not really tell in favour of a debt, but merely in favour of national guarantee, which could equally well be given by other methods, *e.g.*, a national bank of deposit and discount.

55. A. Necessary Functions of Government (*supra*, § 49).

What are the economical evils that follow an improper manner of carrying out the ordinary functions of government?

> I. Imperfect security of person and property discourages labour and frugality and, as it favours the strong at the expense of the weak, generally leads the productive classes, for the sake of protection, to put themselves into voluntary serfdom. On the other hand the example of the free towns of Italy, Flanders and the Hanseatic League, shows that comparative anarchy is not always a bar to economic progress. Difficulties and hardships are often an incentive to exertion.
>
> II. Over-taxation is not so bad in its effects as arbitrary or unfairly distributed taxation, but may check accumulation or drive Capital out of a country before going so far as to discourage industry (*cf.* Holland).
>
> III. Imperfections in the laws generally and the administration of justice, such as "incognoscibility

of the law" (Bentham), delays, vexatious procedure (as in real property law in England which prevents land being easily transferable), are really ramifications of I. English mercantile law is, on the whole, good, being chiefly based on the custom of merchants, and thus made by those most interested in its goodness.

IV. Imperfection in particular laws, especially those relating to—

(i) *Inheritance* (*supra*, § 19, i. and ii., for criticism of general principles). The existing laws operate in different countries in opposite ways—

(*a*) In England, *primogeniture*, supported by *entail*, is the general rule, with the object of keeping land, etc., together in large masses.

(*b*) In France, *equal division* among all children or relations in the same degree of propinquity is the law, and its object is to break down large hereditary fortunes and a landed aristocracy.

(*a*) Has been defended on the grounds—

(1) That it "makes but one fool in a family" Dr. Johnson), but if unearned riches are so pernicious, why have even "one fool?" Perhaps to stimulate the younger sons to industry in the hope of achieving a position like that of their more fortunate brothers. But have not fortunes *earned* by others an even greater effect as a stimulus, and is not besides a diffusion of wealth more desirable than its concentration?

(2) That division of the land diminishes its productive power. Even if this were true (*supra*, § 22, B. ii.) division of the *inheritance* does not necessarily imply division of the *land*.

N.B.—The continuance of entails, by fixing the order of the succession and giving the holder of an estate only a life interest, aims at preventing the holder from burthening his successor. The evils of this system, even when limited as in England, are even greater than those of primogeniture, for the holder of an entailed estate can still ruin himself, is not at all likely to have the means of improving the property and cannot hand it over to anyone who has, since he cannot alienate nor even, till lately, grant long leases.

(b) By interfering with the liberty of bequest postpones a real claim, the owner's liberty of gift, to an imaginary one, the children's legal right, without necessarily achieving its object. For impartial division is not always synonymous with equal division. Some children may be less capable of providing for themselves than others. Litigious coheirs can make trouble which the law cannot equitably remedy. Moreover, such a law makes necessary continuous interference in the concerns of individuals in order to prevent its defeat by alienation *inter vivos*.

(ii) *Contracts.*

(a) Partnerships. [Few things have changed since Mill wrote so much as the law relating to partnerships, so the force of his complaints against anything which tends to impede the formation of large capitals through the aggregation of smaller ones is very much lessened as far as England is concerned. The cumbrous Chancery procedure with regard to partnership accounts has been done away with. Limited Liability Companies (*Sociétés anonymes*) need not, since the Act of 1855, be called into existence by a special act of the legislature or the crown, like the old Chartered Companies; and partnerships in which there may be limited shareholders, acting with others who are responsible with their whole fortunes (partnership *en commandite*), have been permitted since 1907; and "private companies" have grown up under the shelter of the Limited Liability laws and have recently been recognised and regulated by law. In all these extensions of partnership the need for publicity, on which Mill insists, has been fully recognised.]

(*b*) Insolvency. Good laws on this subject are of economical importance, because

(1) The economical well-being of men depends on their being able to trust one another.

(2) Bad debts add to the cost of production.

The laws, therefore, while not being barbarous, should be sufficiently severe to prevent men being able to shuffle off the consequences of their misconduct (for misfortune is very rarely the cause of bankruptcy) and to prevent a curtailment of credit, which is not necessarily an evil, and, even if it were, would only be remedied by a worse one if curtailed by lax bankruptcy laws.

56. B. Optional Functions of Government (*supra*, § 49).

I. Before discussing the general principles of government interference, certain interferences grounded on false theories may be eliminated.

(i) *Protection to Native Industry*, *i.e.*, a prohibition or discouragement by heavy duties of such commodities as are capable of being produced at home. Now no importation takes place without being, economically speaking, a national good, and to prohibit such importation is to render the labour and capital of the country less efficient in production than they would otherwise be (*supra*, § 39). Such policy was originally grounded on the Mercantile System (*supra*, § 2, A.), but even since this has been abandoned many still cling to the restrictive system on the following grounds :—

(*a*) The specious plea of employing our own

countrymen and our national industry. But the alternative is not between employing our own people and foreigners but between employing one class or another of our own people, for an imported commodity is always paid for directly or indirectly with the produce of our own industry.

(*b*) That the Navigation Laws were grounded on the necessity of keeping up a nursery of seamen for the navy. This is a political argument of some value, but when the Navigation Laws had achieved their object (at some economic disadvantage) of destroying the Dutch monopoly of the carrying trade, there was no longer any reason for maintaining this invidious exception to the general rule of Free Trade.

(*c*) That we ought to be independent of foreigners for the food of the people. This is to found a general system of policy on so improbable a danger as that of being at war with all the nations of the world at once, or to suppose that the whole country could be blockaded like a town [!].

(*d*) The great saving in cost of carriage consequent on producing commodities at or near to the place they are to be consumed (Carey). But the cost of such carriage falls not on the producers but on the consumers, and though it is a burthen on the industry of the world it is only borne for more than equivalent advantage.

(*e*) That countries that export agricultural produce actually export a portion of their soil (the argument of earth butchery, Carey). This is really a question of the cost of manuring, *i.e.*, a similar one to that of the cost of carriage.

(*f*) That the superiority of one country over another in a branch of production often arises only from having begun it sooner. This can be conceded in a new country or a new industry. A protecting duty may sometimes be defensible, but then, however, that ought to be strictly limited in point of time, and provision be made that in its later existence it be on a gradually decreasing scale. Such temporary protection is of the same nature as a patent. [Mill afterwards expressed his intention of withdrawing this concession in favour of Protection.]

The main economic arguments for Protection are thus totally invalid, [but it must be remembered that it is the *political* rather than the economic arguments that provide the strongest case for Protection.]

(ii) *Usury Laws*. These mischievous interferences with the spontaneous course of industrial transactions were at first grounded on religious prejudices, drawn from the Jewish Law, and the sanction of the Catholic Church to this prejudice has been one of the reasons for the industrial inferiority of the Catholic, compared with the Protestant, parts of Europe. Even when the taking of interest has not been altogether forbidden it has been usual for Governments to limit the rate. Adam Smith approved of such restrictions, but Bentham's Letters on Usury have changed enlightened opinion on this matter. [At present there is inclined to be a reaction in favour of restrictions.]

Restrictions are imposed from two motives—

(a) For the benefit of the borrowers who are supposed to be at a disadvantage. But why should this be the only bargain a man cannot make without the Law's intermeddling, which indeed may even be to his disadvantage, for when he has not good security to offer he may be driven to make an illegal, and therefore more costly, bargain than necessary?

(b) On the ground that it is for the general good that Interest should be low. This would lead either to the with-holding of loanable Capital, which would make the natural rate of Interest higher, or to the evasion of the law, which would make it higher still.

(iii) *Regulation of Prices.* Governments have often interfered with the freedom of contracts to regulate prices and especially to cheapen the price of food. But since the average price of food conforms to the cost of production, if the law fixes a price below this the producer will not, unless compelled to do so, produce more than he requires for his own consumption. In a case of actual scarcity nothing can give general relief except a determination by the richer classes to diminish their own consumption. If they buy and consume their usual quantity of food and content themselves by giving money they do no good. The price is forced up until the poorest competitors have no longer the means of competing, and the privation of food is thrown exclusively on the indigent, the other classes being only affected pecuniarily. Direct measures at the cost of the State to procure food at a distance are expedient when from peculiar reasons the thing is not likely to be done by private speculation.

(iv) *Monopolies.* A monopoly is an instrument for producing artificial dearness. It enables the holder of the monopoly to levy such an amount of taxation on the public, as will not make the public forego the use of the commodity. Any such limitation of competition may have mischievous effects quite disproportioned to the apparent cause, *e.g.*, the silk manufacture of England remained far behind that of any country of Europe so long as the foreign fabrics were prohibited. In addition to the tax levied for the profit of the monopolists the consumers thus pay an additional tax for their incapacity.

N.B.—The condemnation of monopolies ought not to extend to patents and to copyright.

(v) *Laws against combination of workmen, cf.*, the famous Statute of Labourers, which avowedly aimed at keeping wages low and exhibited the infernal spirit of the slave master. Now wages cannot be maintained above their market rate by combination, but they do not rise to their market rate of themselves. The labourer must ask for the additional amount, and he cannot ask for it effectively except in combination. It is therefore a great error to condemn *per se* and absolutely either *trade unions* or the collective action of *strikes*. It is, however, an indispensible condition of tolerating combinations that they should be voluntary. Attempts to compel workmen to join a union or to take part in a strike by threats or violence should be forbidden.

(vi) *Restrictions on opinion or its publication.* A regime which produces mental slavery like that of the Inquisition is fatal to all prosperity, even of an economic kind; for the human mind when prevented by fear from exercising its faculties freely on important subjects acquires a general torpidity and imbecility.

II. A consideration of the general principles of Government interference must be preceded by a further classification of it into—

(*a*) Authoritative interference, *i.e.*, the ordering that certain things should be done or not done or done in a particular way, and

(*b*) Unauthoritative interference, *i.e.*, leaving individuals free to adopt their own methods, *e.g.*, a Church Establishment, side by side with complete religious toleration.

It is obviously against the former that the following objections to Government interference are chiefly levied.

(i) The compulsory character of intervention is objectionable, because it interferes with the ideal of individual liberty. This objection clearly applies most to (a), but it must be remembered that some form of compulsion is necessary in all Government interference if only for the levying of the funds to support it.

(ii) Every increase of the functions of Government is an increase both of its authority and its influence. Any such increase ought to be regarded with unremitting jealousy, perhaps more in a democracy than any other form of political society, because where public opinion is sovereign the oppressed individual will with difficulty find a rival power to which to appeal for relief.

(iii) An increase of the occupations and responsibilities of Government may not allow sufficient scope for the advantages of the Division of Labour, though this disadvantage may be overcome by good organization, which is improbable in Governments because

(iv) Government officials have less interest in their work than private individuals, and therefore as a rule private agencies show superior efficiency.

(v) A people is at a disadvantage that has everything done for it. It is important as a security against political slavery that there should be a diffusion of an intelligent spirit among the governed. This can best be achieved by allowing them to cultivate habits of collective action among themselves.

Thus we arrive at the conclusion that non-interference or *laisser faire* should be the general rule, but—

III. *Laisser faire* is liable to certain large *exceptions*.

(i) There are cases in which the consumer is an incompetent judge of the commodity. This is particularly so with education; the uncultivated cannot be competent judges of cultivation. With regard to elementary education the exception to ordinary rules may justifiably be carried further, to the extent of making it both compulsory and free, because the cost cannot be paid from the common wages of unskilled labour, and the alternative is therefore private charity or Government provision, and the latter has advantages both in quality and quantity.

(ii) There are cases in which the person most

interested is incapable of judging or acting for himself and is therefore bound to be in the power of others, *e.g.*, idiots, children and the lower animals. They must be protected by Government against the improper conduct of those who have power over them. To include women in this group, however, is both indefensible in principle and mischievous in practice. They both *can* judge for themselves, and, when economically independent, *do* judge for themselves. Women employed in factories are the only women in the labouring rank of life whose position is not that of slaves and drudges.

(iii) Individuals cannot always be regarded as the best judges of their own interests, when they decide irrevocably now what will be best for their interests at some future time. Therefore the practical maxim of leaving contracts free is not applicable without great limitations in case of engagements in *perpetuity*: the Law should be jealous of such engagements, and where it does not permit the parties themselves to revoke them should be prepared to grant a release when a sufficient case is made out before an impartial authority, *cf.* marriage.

(iv) Where the choice is between Government management and management not by all the parties interested, but by a delegated authority, as in the case of joint stock management, the argument against Government interference is greatly weakened. It is argued in such cases that directors are always shareholders, but it must always be remembered that the members of a Government are invariably taxpayers. The argument advanced in II. (v) must of course be taken into consideration, and will lead us to the conclusion that most things which are likely to be even tolerably done by voluntary associations should, generally speaking, be left to them. But it does not follow that the manner in which they do their work should be entirely uncontrolled, especially in the case of practical monopolies, *e.g.*, water, gas, railways.

(v) There are many cases in which public intervention may be necessary to give effect to the wishes of the persons interested, *e.g.*, hours of labour, disposal of Colonial lands.

(vi) The argument that individuals are the best judges of their own interests cannot be used in those cases in which the acts the Government claims to interfere with are done for the interests of other people, *e.g.*, the case of public charity. It is agreed that something must be done to relieve destitution. If this is left to private charity the tendency will be for it to be too lavish at one place and too scanty at another. Besides, if the Government provides subsistence for the criminal poor it would be manifestly putting a premium on crime not to do the same for the poor who have not offended. Hence the necessity for Poor Laws, which should be framed on the general principle that while assistance is available to everybody a strong motive is left to everyone to do without it if he can.

(vii) In some cases the acts done by individuals are intended solely for their own benefit, but have consequences extending indefinitely beyond them to the interests either of the nation or of posterity. To such cases the same general principles apply as in (vi). Thus colonisation can only be made self-supporting by being State aided. [A point which somewhat loses force in Mill's later editions, owing to the large amount of spontaneous emigration from Ireland.] Other examples of a similar kind are voyages of scientific exploration, maintenance of lighthouses, etc., establishment of professorships, and other things desirable for the general interest of mankind or of future generations.

Such are the cases in which the intervention of Government is intrinsically suitable, but it cannot always stop there. It may be that a country is too poor or too backward for private agency, however much more suitable, to do certain works. Government intervention may then be necessary, but a good Government will give all its aid in such a shape as to encourage and nurture any rudiments it may find of a spirit of individual exertion.

QUESTIONS.

The numbers in parenthesis refer to sections.
An asterisk (*) = not for Pass Students.

1. What is Political Economy and how does Mill propose to deal with it? (1 and 4).

2. Define wealth. To what extent are (a) air, (b) a mortgage, and (c) slaves wealth? (1 and 2).

3. Why is it an error to give either labour or land a priority of importance as an agent of production? To what extent has this error appeared in economic theory or practice? (5 and 15).

4. Define productive and unproductive labour, and examine the grounds of the distinction (7).

5. Reconcile the propositions that "Capital is the result of saving" and "whatever is saved is consumed" (9).

6. State and criticise Mill's fundamental propositions concerning Capital (9 and 25 A note).

7. Explain the effects which the introduction of machinery may have upon wages and profits, distinguishing carefully between temporary and permanent effects (10 and 11).

8. What are the principle causes upon which the productiveness of labour depends? (12).

9. Give Mill's criticisms and amplifications of Adam Smith's enumeration of the advantages of division of labour (13).

10. Discuss the respective advantages of production on a small scale (14).

11. Give examples of (a) deficiency, and of (b) excess in the strength of the desire of accumulation, and explain the causes of such diversity (15).

12. Why does the economist draw a distinction between land and other forms of wealth? (15).

13. What was the influence of Malthus' theory of population on Mill's economic views (15 A, 16 B end, and 25).

14. What is meant by the law of diminishing return, and how far does it influence Mill's views upon population? (15 C and 16 B).

15. What important difference is there between the laws of production and the laws of distribution? and to what extent are the latter controlable by mankind? (4 and 17).

16. Examine Mill's attitude towards Socialism in general (18).

17. Are Mill's criticisms of (*a*) St. Simonism and (*b*) Fourierism applicable to modern Socialistic schemes? (18).

*18. What do you suppose would have been Mill's views of Syndicalism? (Syndicalism, starting from the premise that labour is the source of all wealth, aims at giving the workers in any branch of industry the ownership of the means of production and the control of the administration of that branch. Its characteristic method is the general strike (5, 18, 19 and 56 l. v.).

19. Describe the conditions which justify property in land from an economic point of view (19 B iii.).

20. How far does custom regulate (*a*) land tenure, (*b*) prices (21).

21. What are the economic effects of slavery? (22 A and 31, note ii.).

22. What are Mill's arguments in favour of Peasant Proprietorship, and how far do you consider that they hold good in England at the present day? (22 B, and consider the effect on farming of the modern importation of foreign cereals. In Mill's time about $\frac{3}{4}$ of the population were fed from home-grown corn, now only about $\frac{1}{10}$ are).

23. What are the chief disadvantages of (*a*) the Metayer system, and (*b*) Cottier tenancy, and to what extent have the evils of the latter been removed from Ireland since Mill wrote? (23 and 24).

24. Enumerate the popular remedies for low wages. Can you suggest any test of their efficacy? (25 B).

25. Account (*a*) for the difference of wages in different employments, (*b*) for the lower wages usually paid to women (25 C).

26. How far did Mill consider there was a solution of the problem of inadequate wages? (25 B).

*27. Consider the probable economic effects if the State raised the wages of agricultural labourers by 15% (25 B).

28. How far is Mill's analysis of profits acceptable to-day? (26).

29. State and illustrate the circumstances which determine the general rate of profit, particularly noticing those which, in the ordinary progress of society, tend to raise or depress it (26).

*30. To what extent is Mill's exposition of the Ricardian theory of Rent satisfactory? (27).

31. Consider how far the revenue derived by a landed proprietor from improvements, such as drainage, fencing, or agricultural buildings, is of the nature of Profit and how far it is of the nature of Rent (27 B).

32. How far is the doctrine of Rent applicable to actual conditions? (27).

33. Explain the theory that value in exchange is composed of two elements—value in use and difficulty of attainment. In what cases, according to this theory, will "Value in Use" be the sole "regulator" of price? (28, 29).

*34. How far can the distinction between "normal" and "market" values be maintained, and what other distinctions between different kinds of values can you suggest? (28, 29, 30, 31).

35. What do you understand by the Equation of Demand and Supply? (29).

36. What are the functions and desiderata of Money (33 A and B).

37. Show the extent to which the value of money depends on the same principles as those which regulate the value of other commodities (33 C).

38. On what depends the value of:—
   (*a*) A picture by Velasquez (29)
   (*b*) A house (29 and 30)
   (*c*) Silk handkerchiefs (30)
   (*d*) Bread (31)
   (*e*) Wine (30 and 31)
   (*f*) A sovereign (33 C and 41)
   (*g*) A £5 note (33 C and 35)?

39. What is the problem that Bimetallism is supposed to solve? (34).

40. In what ways, if any, does Credit assist (*a*) the production and (*b*) the exchange of wealth (35 and 41).

41. Show the influence of Credit on prices and analyse the phenomena of a commercial crisis (35).

42. Examine the arguments for and against an inconvertible paper currency (36).

43. Why and in what ways does the theory of International value differ from the general theory as to a home product? (39 and 40).

*44. What fixes the price (in English money) of French goods bought by an English merchant? (40 and 43).

45. How far is an "unfavourable balance of trade" really unfavourable? (41).

46. Explain the machinery of international exchange (41 and 43).

47. What causes tend to determine the rate of Interest? (44).

48. What are the arguments for and against the Bank Charter Act of 1844? (45).

49. Distinguish wages and the cost of labour (46 B and 30 III.).

*50. By what arguments does Mill justify his contention that profits tend to fall to a minimum, and what conclusions does he draw from this supposed tendency (48).

*51. Discuss the policy of executing useful public works by means of loans raised by the Government (48).

52. How far does modern taxation in England conform to the principles laid down by Mill? (50).

53. State accurately the distinction between direct and indirect taxation and their respective advantages and disadvantages (51, 52, 53).

54. Is it possible or desirable that taxes should never fall on Capital? (50 E).

55. What did Mill lay down as the requisites for a just Income Tax, and what was the objection he saw to such a tax? How far does the present Income Tax fulfil his desiderata? (50 and 51 A, and 9 D note).

56. What is meant by "incidence of taxation"? Discuss the incidence of the following taxes:—
    (a) On wages (51 A).
    (b) On motor cars (51 B).
    (c) On houses (51 B).
    (d) On windows (51 B).
    (e) On tobacco (52).
    (f) On beet sugar (52)
    (g) On contracts (53).

*57. What are the advantages and disadvantages of a Government retaining its right of property in the soil, and raising its revenue in the form of rent? (50 D and 19 B).

58. Is it desirable to defray extraordinary public expenditure by loans? (54).

59. What were Mill's views as to (a) the creation, (b) the redemption of a National Debt? (54).

60. What cases of Government interference does Mill regard as particularly objectionable? (56 I.).

61. On what grounds and within what limits did Mill defend the principle of *laissez-faire*? (56 II. and III.).

62. Give Mill's views or probable views on:—
    (a) The power of bequest (19).

(b) A super tax on incomes (50 C).
(c) Taxation of unearned increment (50 D).
(d) Primogeniture (55 iv.).
(e) Usury laws (56 i. ii.).
(f) A compulsory Act for Higher Education (56 iii. i.).
(g) State control of the feeble-minded (56 iii. ii.).
(h) State ownership of telephones (56 iii. iv.).
(i) State aid for emigration (56 iii. vii. and 16 B).

63. Explain and comment on :—
(a) Some writers have raised the question, whether nature gives more assistance to labour in one kind of industry or in another (5).
(b) There is a distinction more important to the wealth of the community than even that between productive and unproductive labour: viz., that between labour for the supply of productive and for the supply of unproductive consumption (7).
(c) The distinction between Capital and not-Capital does not lie in the kind of commodities, but in the mind of the Capitalist (8).
(d) Industry is limited by Capital (9 A).
(e) A person does good to labourers, not by what he consumes in himself, but solely by what he does not so consume (9 D).
(f) The division of labour is limited by the extent of the market (13 B).
(g) The advantages of the joint-stock principle are numerous and important (14 A).
(h) Undoubtedly the non-agricultural population will bear a less ratio to the agricultural, under small than under large cultivation. But that it will be less numerous absolutely is by no means a consequence (14 B).
(i) Good roads are equivalent to good tools (15 C ii.).
(j) Unlike the laws of Production, those of Distribution are partly of human institution (17).
(k) A more real difficulty (to Communism) is that of fairly apportioning the labour of the community among its members (17 A).
(l) Landed property is felt, even by those most tenacious of its rights, to be a different thing from other property (19 B).
(m) It would be a great misconception of the actual course of human affairs to suppose that competition exercises in fact this unlimited sway (21).
(n) Whether the proprietors themselves would lose by the emancipation of their slaves is a different question from the

comparative effectiveness of free and slave labour to the community (22 A note).

(o) Yet there are germs of a tendency to the formation of peasant proprietors on Irish soil, which require only the aid of a friendly legislator to foster them (24 B).

(p) Experience has shown the sort of work to be expected from recipients of public charity (25 B).

(q) For the purpose therefore of altering the habits of the labouring people, there is need of a two-fold action, directed simultaneously upon their intelligence and their poverty (25 B).

(r) There are kinds of labour of which the wages are fixed by custom and not by competition.

(s) The rate of profit on Capital in all employments tends to an equality (26 B).

(t) The cost of labour, then, is, in the language of mathematicians, a function of three variables (26 B).

(u) Rent of land is never a part of the cost of production (27 C and 31).

(v) The value of a commodity is not a name of an inherent and substantive quality of the thing itself (28).

(w) The exchange value of a thing may fall short, to any amount, of its value in use; but that it can ever exceed the value in use, implies a contradiction (28 I.).

(x) There cannot be a general rise of values (28 II.).

(y) Supply and Demand are but another expression for reciprocal demand (29 II.).

(z) Monopoly value does not depend on any peculiar principle, but is a mere variety of the ordinary case of Demand and Supply (29 III.).

(A) Although, however, *general* wages, whether high or low, do not affect values, yet if wages are higher in one employment than another, or if they rise or fall permanently in one employment without doing so in others, these inequalities do really operate upon values (30 III).

(B) Cases of extra profit analogous to rent are more frequent in the transactions of industry than is sometimes supposed (31 C iv.).

(C) It is not with money that things are really purchased (33 C).

(D) Money is a commodity, and its value is determined like that of other commodities (33 C).

(E) The phrase, rapidity of circulation, requires some comment (33 C).

(F) But the convenience of business has given birth to an arrangement which makes all the banking-houses of the City of London, for certain purposes, virtually one establishment (35 A. d.).

(G) The example of the *assignats* has been said not to be conclusive, because an *assignat* only represented land in general, but not a definite quantity of land (36 C).

(H) It must be remembered, too, that general high prices, even supposing them to exist, can be of no use to a producer or dealer, considered as such (36 C).

(I) The only direct advantage of foreign commerce consists in the imports (39 B).

(J) "The value of money, in countries where it is an important commodity, must be entirely regulated by its value in the countries which produce it" (41 A).

(K) It remains to observe that the exchanges do not depend on the balance of debts and credits with each country separately (41 B note).

(L) This disinclination, when at its extreme point, is called a panic (44 A ii.).

(M) The rate of interest bears no necessary relation to the quantity or value of the money in circulation (44 B).

(N) General low wages never caused any country to undersell its rivals, nor did general high wages ever hinder it from doing so (46 B).

(O) Exchange, and money therefore, make no difference in the law of rent (47).

*(P) Wherever competition is not, monopoly is (48 end).

(Q) Equality of taxation means equality of sacrifice (50 B).

(R) To tax the larger incomes at a higher percentage than the smaller is to lay a tax on industry and economy (50 C).

(S) They grow richer, as it were in their sleep, without working, risking, or economizing (50 D).

(T) A tax on profits, like a tax on rent, must, at least in its immediate operation, fall wholly on the payer (51 A).

(U) A discriminating duty makes the consumer pay two distinct taxes, only one of which is paid to the Government, and that frequently the less onerous of the two (52).

(V) Those are therefore right who maintain that taxes on imports are partly paid by foreigners; but they are mistaken when they say that it is by the foreign producer (52).

(W) All taxes on international trade tend to produce a disturbance and readjustment of what we have termed the Equation of International Demand (52 v.).

(X) We are often told that taxes on commodities are less burthensome than other taxes, because the contributor can escape from them (53 A).

(Y) These (taxes on luxuries) have some properties which strongly recommend them (53 B).

(Z) The amount is much more certain of fructifying if it is not "left in the pockets of the people" (54 B).

(ZZ) The most effective of these (fallacies) is the specious plea of employing our own countrymen and our national industry instead of feeding and supporting the industry of foreigners (56 I.).

QUESTIONS.

64. Explain or write short notes on the following terms:—

Accommodation Bills (35).
Allotments (25 B).
Arbitration of Exchange (41 B).
Diminishing Return (15 C. 31).
Assignats (36).
Bank Charter Act, 1844 (45).
Banking Theory (45).
Bills of Exchange (35, 41 B).
Bimetallism (34).
Book Credit (35).
Capital (8, 15).
Cheques (35).
Circulating Capital (10).
Combination of Labour (13).
Communism (18).
Conacre (25, 13).
Contract, Taxes on (53).
Cottiers (24).
Credit (35).
Currency Theory (45).
Demand (29).
Direct Taxes (61, 53).
Discriminating Duty (52).
Division of Labour (13).
Economistes (5).
Efficiency of Money (33 C).
Emigration (16 B, 57 III.).
Equation of International Demand (40 B).
Fictitious Bills (35).
Fixed Capital (10).
Fourierism (18).
Graduated Income Tax (50 C).
Grande et Petite Culture (14).
House Tax (51 B).
Impôt progressif (50 C).
Income Tax (51 A).
Inconvertible Paper Money (36).
Indirect Taxes, (51, 53).
Interest (44).
Laissez faire (56).

Law Taxes (53).
Local Taxes (53 D).
Measure of Value (37 B).
Mercantile System (2, 39 B).
Metayer (23).
Money (33).
Monopolies (25 C, 20 III., 57 I.).
National Debt (54).
Navigation Laws (56 I.).
Over-supply (37 A).
Parcelles (14 B).
Peasant Proprietorship (22 B).
Partnership (56).
   ,,   *en commandite* (56).
Poor Laws (25, 56 III.).
Primogeniture (55).
Profits (26).
Promissory Notes (35).
Protection (52, 56).
Rent (27).
Ryots (24).
St. Simonism (18).
Seignorage (33 C).
Slavery (19 B IV., 22 P, 31 *b*).
Socialism (18).
Sociétés anonymes (55).
Strikes (56).
Supply (29).
Token Money (34).
Trade Unions (57).
Ulster Tenant Right (24).
Underselling (46).
Unfavourable Exchange (41).
Unproductive Labour (7).
Usury Laws (56 I.).
Value in Exchange (28).
   ,,   Use (28).
Value of Money (44 B).
Wages (25).
Wages of Superintendence (26).
Wage Fund Theory (9 note, 25 A note).
Window Tax (51 B).
Zemindars (24).

From B. H. BLACKWELL'S LIST.

A Student's Manual of English Constitutional Histo
By D. J. MEDLEY, M.A., Professor of History in the Univer of Glasgow. Fifth Edition, enlarged and revised. Large cr 8vo, *cloth*, 12s. 6d. net.
  "Probably the most complete and thorough handbook of Eng constitutional history now available."—*The Law Quarterly Revie*

A Short Constitutional History of England. By ST. CL FEILDEN. Revised, and in part re-written, by W. GRAY ETH IDGE, M.A. Fourth Edition, revised and brought up to date D. H. J. HARTLEY, M.A. Crown 8vo, *cloth*, 5s. net.
  "A very excellent handbook."—*The Law Students' Journal.*

Worked Exercises in Elementary Geometry. By F. GILLESPIE, M.A. Crown 8vo, *cloth*, 3s. 6d. net.
  The Exercises, which are arranged in logical sequence, designed to cover the ground of the various University Matricula Examinations, the Oxford and Cambridge Local and Joint B Examinations, the Leaving Certificates of the Public Schools, the Schedules of the Training Colleges.

A Short History and Exposition of the Apostles' Cr and of the first eight of the Thirty-nine Articles of Religi
By Rev. E. J. BODINGTON, with a Preface by the late Lo BISHOP OF SALISBURY. Large fcap. 8vo, *cloth*, 3s. 6d.
  "The book deserves every word said in its favour by the Bish of Salisbury."—*The Church Times.*

The French Wars of Religion: their Political Aspec
By E. ARMSTRONG, M.A. An Expansion of Three Lectur delivered before the Oxford University Extension Summ Meeting of August, 1892. Second Edition corrected. Post 8 *cloth*, 3s. 6d. net.
  "Among the best and wisest things that have been said on t subject."—*The Oxford Magazine.*

Analysis of Maine's Ancient Law. With Notes by J. OLDHAM, M.A. Crown 8vo, *sewed*, 1s. net.
  "An excellent little summary for students."—*The Literary Wor*

The Social Compact. A Guide to some Writers on t Science and Art of Politics. By R. W. LEE. Crown 8vo, *sew* 2s. 6d.
  "It cannot but prove useful."—*The Scotsman.*

BROAD STREET, OXFORD.

ImTheStory.com

Personalized Classic Books in many genre's

Unique gift for kids, partners, friends, colleagues

Customize:

- Character Names
- Upload your own front/back cover images (optional)
- Inscribe a personal message/dedication on the inside page (optional)

Customize many titles Including
- Alice in Wonderland
- Romeo and Juliet
- The Wizard of Oz
- A Christmas Carol
- Dracula
- Dr. Jekyll & Mr. Hyde
- And more...

Emily's Adventures in Wonderland

Ryan & Julia

SD - #0098 - 141122 - C0 - 229/152/9 - PB - 9781313200271 - Gloss Lamination